ROMANIA

AN ECONOMIC ASSESSMENT

ORGANISATION FOR ECONOMIC CO-OPERATION AND DEVELOPMENT
CENTRE FOR CO-OPERATION WITH THE EUROPEAN ECONOMIES IN TRANSITION

ORGANISATION FOR ECONOMIC CO-OPERATION AND DEVELOPMENT

Pursuant to Article 1 of the Convention signed in Paris on 14th December 1960, and which came into force on 30th September 1961, the Organisation for Economic Co-operation and Development (OECD) shall promote policies designed:

— to achieve the highest sustainable economic growth and employment and a rising standard of living in Member countries, while maintaining financial stability, and thus to contribute to the development of the world economy;

— to contribute to sound economic expansion in Member as well as non-member countries in the process of economic development; and

— to contribute to the expansion of world trade on a multilateral, non-discriminatory basis in accordance with international obligations.

The original Member countries of the OECD are Austria, Belgium, Canada, Denmark, France, Germany, Greece, Iceland, Ireland, Italy, Luxembourg, the Netherlands, Norway, Portugal, Spain, Sweden, Switzerland, Turkey, the United Kingdom and the United States. The following countries became Members subsequently through accession at the dates indicated hereafter: Japan (28th April 1964), Finland (28th January 1969), Australia (7th June 1971) and New Zealand (29th May 1973). The Commission of the European Communities takes part in the work of the OECD (Article 13 of the OECD Convention).

Hungary and Poland participate in the OECD Programme "Partners in Transition", which is managed by the Centre for Co-operation with European Economies in Transition.

Publié en français sous le titre :

LA ROUMANIE
ÉVALUATION DE LA SITUATION ÉCONOMIQUE

Preface

Although frequently underestimated abroad, Romania has undertaken major structural reforms over the past three years. Romania started from extremely difficult initial conditions – extreme centralisation, a high degree of autarky, and no experience of partial reforms such as those undertaken in other central and eastern European economies during the 1980s. Today the legal infrastructure for a market economy has now been largely established, agriculture has been privatised, a private sector is emerging in other sectors, trade has been liberalised and the framework of an ambitious mass privatisation programme is nearly complete. The macroeconomic performance has, however, been disappointing, offsetting these impressive achievements: the collapse in output is now longer and deeper than in most other countries in transition, inflation remains very high and there is a chronic shortage of foreign currency. Unlike in other reforming economies, exports are only slowly emerging as a growth factor.

This report provides a focused analysis of the background to the current situation and attempts to identify policy choices that are important for overcoming the serious macroeconomic situation. It pays close attention to the manner in which structural reforms have been introduced and the way in which these have interacted with the conduct of stabilization policy.

Romania faces a particularly difficult situation. Structural reform has been intentionally gradual with a great deal of emphasis given to avoiding social cost. While laudable, the goal has sometimes led to a lack of coherence between structural reforms and stabilization, and delays in implementation, as interest groups have sought to protect their own positions. An important consequence has been that price liberalisation remains incomplete and state enterprises are not financially disciplined, undermining policy credibility and requiring continued administrative intervention and subsidies. Expectations of further price liberalisation have helped maintain a high level of inflation expectations. These have interacted with the exchange rate to produce a dangerous inflation/devaluation cycle with little structural improvement in the balance of payments or output. This report argues that a determined effort is now necessary to rapidly complete price liberalisation, stabilize the exchange rate, and accelerate those structural reforms which would improve financial discipline of enterprises. Western assistance will be vital if the balance of payments situation is to be prevented from slowing the needed structural reforms.

Since this report was completed, the government has introduced (in March 1993) a wide-ranging programme for structural reform and macroeconomic stabilization. While this programme is not fully analyzed here, those elements which were public knowledge in January 1993 are taken into consideration.

The governmental programme, if fully implemented, would go some distance to meeting the recommendations of this assessment. It focuses on structural reforms to make monetary and fiscal policy more effective. The reforms include enforcement of legislation to strengthen the financial discipline of firms and measures to deal with the large inter-enterprise arrears by transferring the debt of the largest loss-making firms from the banks to a new restructuring body. Priority is also given to the promotion of competition: specific measures include the introduction of a new competition law and a tighter regulatory environment for state-owned monopolies (''régies autonomes''). The remaining controls over prices and margins will be progressively liberalised during the life of the government.

The hope is that this report will contribute to a better understanding of the situation of the Romanian economy and thus foster support for the steps now required if Romania is to fulfil the enormous natural and human potential which it possesses.

Salvatore Zecchini
OECD Assistant Secretary General
Director of the CCEET

Foreword

This report was prepared in the OECD Economics Department as part of the general work programme of the OECD Centre for Co-operation with European Economies in Transition (CCEET). It was discussed at a seminar organised by the CCEET on 26 March 1993 with the participation of experts and policy makers from Romania and experts from OECD Member countries and major international institutions. The main points of this discussion are summarised at the end.

The report aims at analysing the reform strategy of Romania in its transition towards a market-based economy. In particular, it focuses on a number of structural problems, such as price reform and financial discipline in state enterprises. The findings of this analysis are the basis for some policy suggestions as well as for highlighting particular areas in which assistance is most appropriate.

Appreciation and thanks are expressed to the Romanian officials and experts who helped in gathering the necessary information and in discussing the issues. The report does not necessarily, however, reflect the views of the Romanian authorities. The report was prepared by Grant Kirkpatrick, Richard Kohl and Val Koromzay of the Economics Department and the summary of the discussion by Scott Thomas of the CCEET. It is published on the responsibility of the Secretary-General.

Table of contents

Tables

Annex I

Annex II

Annex III

Figures

Annex II

9

I. The Romanian Reform Programme in Perspective

The initial conditions for reform facing Romania at the end of 1989 were extremely difficult. The economic structure was highly distorted, implying large output losses with any shift to world prices and consumer sovereignty; and the need for a massive reallocation of resources. Lacking experience with the sorts of partial liberalisations undertaken in other parts of central and eastern Europe in the 1970s and 1980s, and with very limited contact with the West, enterprises and government were unprepared to judge policy tradeoffs in the reform process, or to design and implement a reform plan. The population had already experienced "shock therapy" through the savage compression of consumption of the 1980s, and was neither materially nor psychologically prepared for continued cut-backs. Politically, the timing and nature of the Romanian Revolution meant the new government had a domestic mandate to initiate a transition to a market economy only if this did not involve social cost; consequently, a gradual approach to market reform was adopted and implemented, since it was believed to provide protection for incomes and to prevent social dislocation. The manner in which the reform has been implemented created scepticism abroad about the commitment of the government to reform, so that foreign support has been inconsistent, with negative repercussions on the domestic reform process. In sum, when compared to most other reforming countries of central and eastern Europe (CEECs), Romania had one of the longest ways to go towards a market economy, but was the least equipped sociologically and politically to get there.

The legacy of communism

Under communism, Romania never had a real period of political or economic liberalisation. It remained committed to the pre-war Soviet model of economic development based on strict autarky, central planning and investment in industry. Over the postwar period this transformed Romania from a largely rural and agricultural country to an economy dominated by heavy industry. By the 1980s, 60 per cent of output was accounted for by industry, producing a complete range of goods, with producer goods accounting for 75 per cent of industrial output. Industry was largely composed of enormous vertically- and horizontally-integrated firms – over 49 per cent of production was accounted for by firms of 3 000 employees or more. Like the composition of output, industrial location was determined by political and not efficiency considerations, and in many districts one firm accounted for the majority of employment. Much of production was highly energy-intensive by Western standards, and concentrated in energy-intensive industries like oil refining, chemicals, metallurgy, and machinery. Production and especially exports were essentially based on the transformation of cheap energy – initially

11

Romania's own large reserves of natural gas and oil, and, as these were depleted, imports of fuel and electricity from other COMECON members.

Corresponding to the emphasis on heavy industry, investment demand rose steadily over the decades, reaching 30 per cent of GDP by 1970. In the 1970s this emphasis was pursued with even greater vigour, so that by 1980 the investment rate was over 35 per cent. This investment drive focused on the importation of Western technology, financed by foreign borrowing from Western commercial banks. In the early 1980s, terms of trade shocks and the inability to translate this investment into hard currency exports engendered a debt crisis and the termination of lending by Western financial institutions.

Other CEECs reacted at the time to the problems of stagnating output and meeting foreign debt payments by experimenting with partial liberalisation: decentralisation and increasing economic incentives. The opposite happened in Romania: under the Ceausescu regime planning was hyper-centralised in the hands of the ruling family, and political

Table 1. **Selected demographic indicators**

	1980	1985	1989	1990	1991
Population characteristics					
Total population (mn, at 1 July)	22.2	22.7	23.2	23.2	23.2[1]
Population growth rate	0.7	0.4	0.4	0.2	−0.1
Number of employed persons (mn)	10.4	10.6	10.9	10.8	10.8
Population density per km^2	93.5	95.7	97.5	97.7	97.6
Life expectancy at birth (years[2])					
Women	71.8	72.7	72.4	72.7	73.1
Men	66.7	66.8	66.5	66.6	66.6
Population death rate (per cent)	1.04	1.09	1.07	1.06	1.09
Infant mortality (under 1 year)	29.3	25.6	26.9	26.9	22.7
Food, health and nutrition					
Calorie intake (calories per day)	3 259	3 057	2 949	3 038	2 832
Population per physician (excl. dentists)	678	567	552	555	551
Population per hospital bed	114	112	112	112	112
Access to safe water (% of pop.)					
Rural	..	..	16	16	16
Urban	..	..	100	100	100

	Years		
	1989-90	1990-91	1991-92
Education			
Percentage of population between 15 and 18 years in school	85.7	72.8	64.9
Primary school enrolment (per cent)	94.6	90.8	90.5

	1980	1985	1989	1990	1991
GDP per capita (US$ at commercial exchange rate for exports)	2 446	1 336	1 571	1 257	1 137

1. The 7 January 1992 census registered 22.8 million.
2. Average of previous three years.
Source: National Commission for Statistics.

repression increased. This was unsuccessful in increasing exports or in reviving output. Instead, the regime attempted to solve the balance of payments problem by a dramatic compression of imports, eliminating imports of new Western technology and deferring maintenance on existing capital. To sustain production in the face of declining total factor productivity, the regime increased inputs to heavy industry, particularly electrical energy, while diverting resources away from the population and unfavoured sectors such as agriculture. The policies of the 1980s were ultimately unsuccessful: by the end of the decade the economy was exhausted and GDP declined in both 1988 and 1989. On the contrary, these policies reinforced the structural distortions of the economy and the energy intensity of industry, depleted the country's energy resources, and dramatically lowered the living standards of the population.[1] The only positive aspect was that foreign debt was repaid ahead of schedule, leaving the country debt-free, but poor.

The legacy of the Ceausescu years had important social and cognitive implications for the reform process. In the aftermath of the Revolution, many Romanians believed that all that was necessary for a revitalisation of the economy and consumption was the removal of repressive economic controls. Romanians at all levels failed to comprehend that a great deal of investment had been simply wasted: that the product of years of forced savings and sacrifice might be nearly worthless at world energy prices. The population was also understandably intent on recovering from the brutal compression of living standards, and was little prepared either materially or psychologically for renewed sacrifice, high unemployment, and the wrenching dislocations of an economy in transition, placing severe limits on a process which would be difficult anywhere. Similarly, the lack of any pre-existing political or economic liberalisation meant that enterprise managers and government technocrats had little experience with economic reform or exposure to economic practice abroad, leading to sometimes inconsistent and contradictory policies and practices.

Finally, the nature of the Romanian Revolution itself has set limits on the reform process. Unlike Poland, for example, there was no pre-existing movement with a policy programme and political legitimacy based on its opposition to the old regime which could take power. The Council of National Salvation which emerged in the days after the spontaneous Revolution was a haphazard, self-appointed coalition which included Communists, military officers, intellectuals, liberals and conservatives. The development of effective democratic government took time, and in the beginning Romanian politics was beset by instability, culminating in the forced resignation of the government of Petre Roman at the end of 1991 in the face of demonstrations by coal miners. As a result of this period of uncertainty, the Romanian Revolution's relative lateness in the context of the collapse of communism, and the lack of a coherent policy programme, the successive governments have not enjoyed the international economic support of the sort extended to Poland.

The progress of reform since the Revolution

The immediate economic goal of the government that came to power in December 1989 was to restore living standards. A number of populist measures were quickly introduced in 1990, including distribution of some land to peasants, reduction in the work week, and diversion of energy away from industry to the population. The result of these policies and the general decompression of the economy was an explosion of consumption and a dramatic drop in investment and industrial production. The imbalance between demand and supply was met by imports, financed by exhausting foreign exchange reserves. GDP dropped for the third straight year, and by year end inflation began accelerating in the face of demand pressures.

In 1991 a macroeconomic stabilization plan was introduced along with a programme of structural reforms which had been developed over the previous year. The hallmark of the structural reform programme was its commitment to gradualism. This was based on the belief that gradual reform, in particular of prices, was the only way of protecting jobs and meeting basic needs during the transition. Price liberalisation was conceived as a phased series of partial reforms that allowed for continued, though diminishing, direct intervention to assure the supply of raw materials to industry and essential goods to the population – while preventing gouging by monopolies, speculators, or both. Enterprise reform was seen as a two-stage process: decentralisation to be followed by sufficient investment and restructuring to allow for privatisation without loss of jobs or production.

Progress on structural reform has been substantial. Two of the most significant achievements have been the privatisation of agriculture and small businesses. The government has largely sold off or leased businesses in services and retail trade to private agents. Agriculture has been decollectivised with an emphasis on restitution to previous owners, recreating a class of small-holding peasants, though the distribution of titles is lagging. State-owned banks and enterprises were decentralised, about half (in value terms) converted into state-managed monopolies ("régies autonomes"), and the other half converted to commercial companies subject to state-appointed boards of directors. A framework for privatisation has been set up, with ownership in commercial companies split 70-30 between a State Ownership Fund and five Private Ownership Funds. A series of price reforms have been implemented: many prices have been completely liberalised and others have been repeatedly reset at world market levels following successive rounds of devaluation – but a number still remain subject to direct control or supervision, usually based on the principle of limits on mark-up pricing. Progress has been made in cleaning up the balance sheets of banks and state enterprises in several rounds of debt forgiveness. A new constitution and the legal basis for a market economy have been created, though new bankruptcy and competition laws have yet to be passed.

Macroeconomic stabilization policies pursued during 1991 and 1992 aimed to stabilize inflation by reducing the monetary overhang and thereafter to maintain a low rate of growth in money and credit. This inflation-control policy was supported by partial wage indexation and an excess wage tax. Tight control over budget deficits was likewise to be maintained; and in 1992 a policy of positive real interest rates was initiated. Exchange rate policy goals remained unclear; the authorities believed that using the exchange rate as a nominal anchor was impossible without either foreign exchange reserves or a stabilization fund, but nevertheless still viewed it as an essential instrument in controlling inflation. At the same time, a general goal of eventually achieving internal convertibility of the lei was also adopted.

Over this period Romania has achieved most of its programmed targets for macroeconomic policy instruments. Despite periods when credit objectives were temporarily abandoned to deal with inter-enterprise arrears or other symptoms of financial distress, the money supply has shrunk steadily in real terms, and any monetary overhang appears to have been eliminated. Monetary policy has, however, been undercut by the use of large amounts of low-interest credits to specific sectors. Less success has been met in establishing positive real interest rates, in part because inflation has continued to run ahead of projections. While the policy aim of keeping the budget more or less in balance has been largely achieved, this has been done at the cost of imposing a heavy tax burden on state enterprises. Moreover, the success in achieving small recorded deficits has been partly undermined by the growing use of off-budget funds. At the same time the composition of state spending has shifted heavily from financing investment to social protection, particularly in the form of rising subsidies to consumers for food and energy. As regards the exchange rate, government efforts to use it as a nominal brake on inflation by keeping it fixed above market-clearing levels have not been successful: repeated devaluations have been necessary in the face of critical foreign exchange shortages. Foreign exchange reserves remain seriously inadequate.

Macroeconomic performance was disappointing in 1991 and 1992, and the situation remains difficult. GDP fell in both years by a cumulative 28.4 per cent, and average real wages have fallen by a larger amount. Even greater recorded output falls would have occurred had enterprises not built up large inventories of goods that had no markets. Private sector activity in trade, services, construction and self-sufficient agriculture has grown rapidly, but – even if substantially underestimated – has not been able to offset the decline in industry. Unemployment, still low by comparison with other CEECs, has risen to over 9 per cent from zero at the start of the reform programme. Inflation, although stabilizing, has continued at around 150-200 per cent annually, undermining confidence in the currency, and internal convertibility of the lei has not been established despite a series of devaluations which have cumulatively reduced the nominal value of the lei by some fifteen fold. Inter-enterprise arrears remain a very serious problem, despite government attempts to clear them, causing disruption of the payments mechanism and contributing to the decline in output. The current account remains in deficit, though export performance improved significantly in the course of 1992. Shortages, though much alleviated, continued to exist in 1991 and 1992 for some key food items, spare parts, raw materials and energy. Despite the privatisation of agriculture, the former breadbasket of Eastern Europe remains a net food importer.

Assessment

The poor performance of the Romanian economy since 1990 is largely a legacy of the Ceausescu regime, but has been worsened in both degree and duration by the manner in which the commitment to gradual structural reform has been implemented. In particular, policy has been characterised by insufficient coherence, credibility and transparency. The fundamental cause of this state of affairs has been the very narrow and short-term orientation given to the meaning of social cost; in practice this has often justified support for existing interests, although the manner in which this has been achieved has evolved in line with the reform process. The consequence has been reversals and backtracking in the implementation of structural reform, inconsistencies between structural reform and stabilization measures, and inconsistencies in stabilization policy. Foremost has been the partial and contradictory nature of price reforms and, closely related, the failure to significantly improve the financial discipline of state enterprises. Continued price controls, price supervision and administrative allocation, especially of some key raw materials and energy – justified by reference to the need to minimise social costs – have limited the role of prices as an allocation mechanism in key sectors of the economy. This has not only delayed the adaptation of enterprises to market conditions but has also created strengthened resistance to structural reforms which has manifested itself in a lack of policy coherence and transparency.

The lack of financial discipline has undermined monetary policy: continued production for inventories has been financed by write-offs of bad debts, subsidised credit, on- and off-budget subsidies, and an explosion of inter-enterprise and tax arrears. This has impaired confidence in the lei, creating an insatiable demand for foreign currency as a store of value and preventing the establishment of currency convertibility. The lack of convertibility and continued price controls have meant that relative prices remain distorted and are partially disconnected from world prices and competition. They have also been very unstable, subjected to differentiated shocks from repeated exchange rate devaluations and delays in the refixing of controlled prices. Devaluations have served to confirm expectations of high inflation, but have not served to strengthen the balance of payments because they have limited effects on import demand for firms facing soft budget constraints. Also, the exchange rate has played only a limited role in allocating scarce foreign exchange: large, unprofitable, energy intensive firms continue to consume valuable resources via allocations of foreign exchange. For fiscal policy, the small recorded budget deficit does not include significant off-budget expenditures and subsidised credits.

This assessment, though negative, does need to be seen clearly in the context of the very difficult initial conditions faced by the authorities in post-Ceausescu Romania. Gradualism may have been the only viable choice in these conditions and – for the reasons summarised below – it was perhaps inevitable that implementation of reform would be beset by problems of incoherence and loss of direction. Economically, amongst the CEECs Romania entered the path to market reform with the greatest structural distortions in terms of concentration on heavy industry and energy intensity, so that it faced the greatest incipient fall in income. Cognitively, the lack of experience with partial liberalisation or knowledge of market economies meant that state planners and industry managers had very limited knowledge with which to design and implement a reform plan. The population, following the barbaric conditions of the late 1980s, was fundamentally conservative in its desire to restore and protect living standards, and correspondingly unprepared to take a leap into the future. For the governments which filled the power vacuum left immediately after the Revolution, these conditions generated an understandable obsession with ensuring the population enough food, heat, hot water and electricity to survive the winter and with preventing mass unemployment and potentially a social explosion. Implementing thorough-going reform was perhaps of necessity subject to the constraints of ensuring social protection, and the lack of consistent financial or political support for reform from the West exacerbated this. Not surprisingly, when confronted by pathological behaviour characteristic of fledgeling markets not yet operating efficiently, the authorities reacted by direct interventions rather than seeking to solve the problems by furthering reforms. In this context, the reforms which have been achieved are significant, but continued gradualism is leading to mounting costs. A concerted effort to accelerate structural reform and allow market behaviour to become established is now needed if the conditions for a supply response and sustained growth are to be put in place.

The rest of this study is divided into four chapters. Chapter II provides a review of the developments in the Romanian economy between 1990 and 1992. Chapter III discusses the evolution of structural reforms and microeconomic policy. This review is not exhaustive, but focuses on areas essential for the establishment of a market economy: price reform and corporate governance. The course of macroeconomic policies is taken up in Chapter IV, where the interaction of policy instruments with microeconomic distortions is stressed. Particular attention is paid to the exchange rate regime and the need for overall policy consistency. Finally, Chapter V presents the main conclusions focusing on the way ahead for Romania in the next phase of its transition to a market economy. Three annexes to this study discuss, respectively, aspects of the accounting system, the agricultural sector, and plans for large-scale privatisation.

II. Macroeconomic Developments 1990-1992

Macroeconomic developments in Romania during 1990-1992 have broadly resembled those experienced in other CEECs, although there are a number of features which are specific to Romania. Output and investment have fallen over the period, although the scale and duration are more pronounced than in most other countries (Figure 1). As in other countries, the associated adjustment of employment has been delayed so that productivity has fallen. Measured real wages are nearly 40 per cent lower than at the outset of the reform process, a development broadly in line with other countries. Inflation remains high and prone to bouts of acceleration and this pattern is more pronounced than in most other countries.

Against these broad similarities, there are a number of significant differences in outcomes which suggest that the economic forces at work in Romania have been different to some extent. The period as a whole has been characterised by chronic shortages of imported intermediate inputs – energy and raw materials in particular – associated with a

Figure 1. **GDP GROWTH IN CENTRAL AND EASTERN EUROPEAN COUNTRIES**

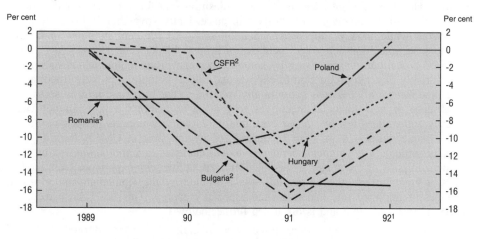

1. OECD projections, except Romania (preliminary estimates).
2. Pre-1991 figures refer to net material product.
3. 1992 GDP in prices of 1991.
Sources: OECD Economic Outlook No. 53 and Romanian National Commission for Statistics.

lack of internal convertibility of the lei. Market-clearing prices were not established for all products, so that queuing and administrative allocation remained pervasive. Inventories have continued to accumulate and there has not been a period of substantial destocking such as took place in most reforming countries after the onset of reform. Until the first half of 1992, exports to the OECD area did not increase, in contrast to other countries where exports emerged early in the transition process as an important growth factor. Finally, the exchange rate has depreciated to a greater extent than elsewhere. In sum, market forces were not permitted to fully overcome the "shortage economy" symptoms characteristic of the previous central planning regime. The persistence of many of these symptoms throughout 1992 suggests that the economic basis for a sustained upturn might still be lacking.

The development of output: sources and uses

The downward trend of GDP which had been apparent since 1987 became more marked during 1990 with GDP falling by around 6 per cent (Table 2). After increasing during the first three months of 1990, industrial production plunged by around 24 per cent by December relative to one year earlier (Figure 2). By contrast, value-added in the agricultural sector increased by some 15 per cent, although gross production decreased by 3 per cent.[2] While output fell, aggregate demand rose: absorption increased 11 per cent, led by consumption and inventory accumulation, the latter accounting for as much as 14 percentage points of the rise in total demand. Offsetting these elements, fixed investment fell by 38 per cent. The combination of increased absorption and decreased production led to a dramatic swing in the current account in convertible currency: from a surplus of 2.5 billion dollars in 1989 to a deficit of 1.7 billion dollars in 1990, a movement of about 13 per cent of GDP.

Economic developments in 1990 reflect certain features specific to that year, which became much less relevant later on. It was a transition year for microeconomic reforms, and a stabilization framework was not yet in place. Until November 1990, most prices were fixed while money supply expanded by some 20 per cent in order to finance inventory accumulation and wage increases of around 14 per cent. Household incomes increased faster than wages, rising by some 26 per cent. Regulations which had previously forcibly directed production to exports and import compression were lifted; at the same time the work week was substantially reduced in the important mining sector.[3] In the absence of new financial incentives to replace regulation,[4] exports in both hard currency and roubles fell by 45 per cent, and hard currency imports jumped by 33 per cent in value terms – more than accounted for by the shift in CMEA trade to hard currency settlement at (higher) world prices. The increase in imports was led by food products; imports of raw materials declined. Indeed, in line with experience from the late 1980s, a great deal of the output fall was attributed by the Romanian authorities to shortages of imported raw materials, and especially energy. This has been a recurrent theme in 1991 and 1992 and is discussed further below.

Beginning in November 1990, prices were liberalised in stages through 1991 and 1992 and a stabilization framework was introduced in early 1991. Stabilization policies are taken up in Chapter IV, and need only be summarised here. The stabilization programme had as its immediate goal to reduce the monetary overhang and to avoid an inflationary spiral which might be initiated by the successive rounds of price liberalisa-

Table 2. **Sources and uses of GDP**

1990 prices

	1989[1]	1990[1]	1991[2]	1992[3]
	(mn lei)	(percentage growth)		
Sources				
Material sectors				
Industry	501 750	−13.5	−25.3	−22.5
Construction	45 557	1.1	−15.5	−9.9
Agriculture & forestry	134 464	15.4	−6.6	−8.7
Transportation & communication	71 232	−23.7	−23.5	−16.1
Trade	54 598	6.2	−9.1	−17.1
Other[4]	22 470	−5.4	18.5	−24.6
Total	830 071	−7.2	−18.4	−18.0
Non-material sectors				
Personal & business services	23 185	4.7	19.5	0.1
Health, social & cultural services	34 945	13.7	8.5	−14.2
Local government & other services	21 001	14.0	17.8	17.5
Total	79 131	11.1	14.1	−1.1
GROSS DOMESTIC PRODUCT	909 202	−5.6	−15.4	−15.4
Uses				
Consumption	623 872	8.9	−22.6	−8.8
Personal consumption[5]	515 904	8.1	−22.4	−10.5
Public consumption	107 968	12.8	−23.4	−1.8
Gross fixed investment	263 651	−35.6	−29.4	−18.9
Stockbuilding (mn lei)	−38 214	89 664	114 400	265 200[3]
Domestic absorption	849 309	10.6	−19.0	−14.5
Net exports of goods & non-factor services	24 947	−425.0	39.1	−7.2
GROSS DOMESTIC PRODUCT	874 256	−1.9	−15.1	−15.4

1. The figures for 1989 and 1990 represent final revisions to the national accounts.
2. Provisional data.
3. Preliminary estimates; prices of 1991.
4. Research and data processing.
5. Including social benefits in kind.
Source: National Commission for Statistics.

tion. To this end, money and credit growth were tightly limited so as to generate a sharp decline in real money and credit balances. Thus, for 1991, the target rate of growth for money was 15 per cent against an expected inflation rate of 160 per cent. While these targets were not met, real money supply nevertheless did decrease by some 60 per cent. During 1992 a further decrease in the real money supply of around 25 per cent was programmed. While credit was to be tightly rationed, nominal interest rates were kept low and highly negative in real terms, until May of 1992, when they were raised sharply. Corresponding to the lack of an active interest rate policy was the absence of an explicit exchange rate goal. In fact the exchange rate regime has been altered on a number of occasions, most importantly at the end of 1991 and again in May 1992. From the fiscal side, the objective was to maintain the deficit in the range of 2-3 per cent.[5]

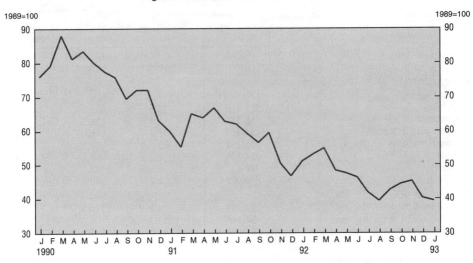

Figure 2. **INDUSTRIAL PRODUCTION**

N. B. Total physical production, unadjusted for number of working days.
Source: National Commission for Statistics.

A further fall in output accompanied the changed policy regime. GDP fell by 15.4 per cent in 1991 and again in 1992. Industrial production also fell in both years (23 per cent and 13 per cent respectively). Value-added in agricultural production fell by 7 per cent in 1991 and, following a severe drought, declined by some 9 per cent in 1992. However, the aggregate situation in agriculture masks the fact that for a number of agricultural activities, production has increased. This contrasts with industry, where production falls have been registered in all sectors. Some recovery in industrial production appears to have taken place in the last months of 1992, though there are indications that this has more to do with inventory building linked to accelerated credit expansion, and possibly seasonal factors, than with any fundamental reversal of trend.

Absorption fell in 1991 by 19 per cent and again in 1992 by some 15 per cent. In 1991 final demand fell more sharply, with consumption and investment decreasing by around 22 and 29 per cent respectively, but stock building once again increased, limiting the decline in overall demand. Associated with inventory accumulation on this scale was a dramatic increase in inter-enterprise arrears during the second half of the year: by October 1991, these arrears had reached 1 trillion lei, in comparison to bank credit to the non-government sector of 800 billion lei. In line with the fall in absorption, imports also decreased sharply, so that even with continued declines in exports, the negative contribution of net exports to GDP narrowed substantially.

The decline in absorption in 1992 was led by a further reduction in investment of around 19 per cent. The contraction of consumption, and especially in public consumption, was very much lower than in 1991: 8 per cent in comparison with 23 per cent in 1991. Stockbuilding continued, though at a slower rate, thus providing less of an offset to continued declines in consumption and investment. With respect to inventory accumulation, the time pattern has been highly uneven: in the opening months of 1992 inventories may have declined only to grow again after the first quarter. Inter-enterprise arrears – after being eliminated in December 1991 – once again increased, reaching in October the levels of late 1991 in nominal terms, although in real terms this represents a 50 per cent decrease from the previous peak. In contrast to previous years, export performance improved, particularly in the second and third quarters, following substantial exchange rate changes; in the first half, the dollar value of exports rose 28 per cent in comparison with 1991.

Inflation and the exchange rate

Inflation over the period has been high and variable; with the exception of the price surge in November 1990, the monthly rate of CPI inflation has averaged around 8 per cent, while for producer prices the rate has at times been close to zero. By December 1992 the price level had risen by some 1 300 per cent in comparison to October 1990. The liberalisation of prices has been a fundamental element of the structural reform programme in Romania, but the pace has been gradual: prices have been adjusted and liberalised on a number of occasions, but the process has also been accompanied by policy reversals. Often the emphasis has been on adjusting prices to world levels rather than simply freeing them to clear markets. The approach has been motivated by the desire both to hold down the rate of inflation and also maintain living standards.

The phased nature of price liberalisation was the main factor influencing the at times divergent evolution of consumer and producer prices. Partial wage indexation to consumer prices introduced a dynamic element to the process. The November 1990 price reforms permitted an explosion in producer prices, but excluded many consumer goods – even though compensation was paid to wage earners at that time. Liberalisation of some consumer prices continued during the first quarter of 1991, which partly explains the higher rate of consumer price inflation in the first quarter. This in turn led to higher nominal wages and a tendency towards accelerating producer price inflation in the second half of the year. Producer price increases were sharply curtailed from March to September 1992 by administrative action to control input prices and margins. Consumer prices continued to rise, feeding through into higher nominal wages. A major adjustment of input prices in the last quarter of 1992 led to a surge in producer prices. As this feeds through, consumer prices and nominal wages will again come under increased pressure.

The gradual nature of price liberalisation has had an important but deleterious impact on the dynamics of inflation. Each price liberalisation was associated with an unexpectedly large surge in the price level. While these surges were only temporary, the rate of inflation between liberalisation episodes has remained high and variable, and this despite the fact that the real money supply has generally been held on a declining trend. More importantly, expected future jumps in the price level associated with either pre-announced liberalisation, or expectations that it must occur, have stimulated agents to seek to defend the real value of their wealth by accumulating goods or foreign exchange. Such behaviour was also encouraged by the maintenance of low interest rates up until May 1992. The result has been continued pressure on the exchange rate and inflation.

A central feature of the Romanian experience has been the continuing depreciation of the exchange rate: over the whole period to the end of 1992 the official rate has

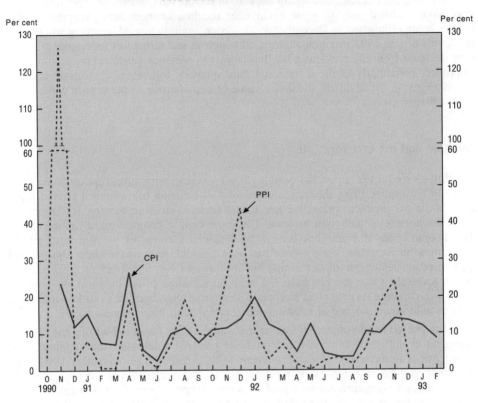

Figure 3. **MONTHLY RATES OF CONSUMER AND PRODUCER PRICE INFLATION**

Source: National Commission for Statistics.

depreciated some 22 fold (Figure 4).[6] The phased devaluation of the official rate has sometimes been taken as an indicator that causality extended from the rate of inflation to the exchange rate. In consequence, phased price deregulation was viewed as helping to stabilize the rate of exchange. This was one rationale behind the price controls which were operative in 1992. The evidence, however, suggests another interpretation. Throughout the period the official rate has remained below the "free market" rate, while foreign exchange has generally remained scarce and often administratively allocated. Eventually the official rate has had to be depreciated in the direction of the unofficial rate. The determinants of the latter are complex but appear to include the uncertainty about the course of price liberalisation and the rate of return on lei assets. Thus, following the increase in interest rates in May 1992, the two exchange rates converged. However, from the end of November, the unofficial rate depreciated strongly (from around 430 lei to the dollar to 700-750 in early 1993) as uncertainty grew about the course of further price liberalisation. The inability to control the exchange rate in turn has rebounded on the development of domestic prices and the inflation rate.[7]

Figure 4. **THE DEVELOPMENT OF THE OFFICIAL AND FREE-MARKET EXCHANGE RATES**

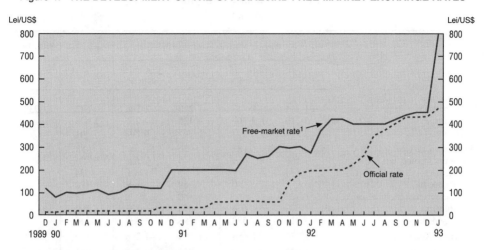

1. The "free-market" rate should only be regarded as indicative and is drawn from various sources; from April-October 1991 it refers to the inter-bank rate and for 1992 it generally refers to the rate at private exchange offices.
Sources: National Bank of Romania and various publications.

The importance of expectational factors in driving the exchange rate, and in turn the development of inflation, derives in part from the lack of financial discipline which has characterised the enterprise sector in Romania. Money supply has remained relatively tight and this should have had a dampening role on inflation, both directly and through the exchange rate. However, enterprises have found ways of circumventing liquidity constraints – for instance by not paying taxes or creditors – and this has weakened the forces which would normally dampen the exchange rate/inflation spiral.

Trade and balance of payments

With low foreign reserves and limited access to international capital markets, Romania has been heavily dependent on international financial assistance during 1991-1992. Though at the end of 1989 Romania had practically no foreign debt and significant foreign exchange reserves, the collapse of the convertible currency account in 1990 reduced reserves by 1.6 billion dollars to less than 400 million dollars, enough for only a few weeks' imports in 1990. During 1991-1992, financing of the trade deficit has been accomplished entirely by short-term trade credits and international financial assistance – particularly from the Bretton Woods institutions and the G24. Despite low levels of debt, Romania has not been able to raise medium- and long-term finance from commercial banks and the world capital markets. The contribution of services and transfers to the balance of payments has been minimal[8] while foreign investment flows remain limited. Medium- and short-term capital flows are expected to be greater in 1992 although an important financing gap will remain, which is expected to be filled in part by

Table 3. **Balance of payments**

Million US$

	1990		1991		Through 30.09.92 [2]	Prov. 1992 [2]
	Total [1]	Convertible currency	Total [1]	Convertible currency		
Trade balance	−3 344	−1 743	−1 220	−1 266	−682	−938
Exports, f.o.b.	5 770	3 364	4 125	3 236	2 679	
Imports, f.o.b.	9 114	5 107	5 345	4 502	3 361	
Balance on services	90	87	36	n.a.	−88	
Interest income, net	160	1	−4	n.a.	−76	
Receipts	174	1	85	n.a.	34	
Payments	14	0	89	n.a.	110	
Other services income, net [3]	−70	86	40	0	−12	
Receipts	749	674	838	831	504	
Payments	819	588	798	831	516	
Current account	−3 254	−1 656	−1 184	−1 266	−770	
Capital account	1 079	10	902	564	981	
Direct foreign investment, net	−18	−18	37	37	46	
Medium- & long-term credits	58	80	257	255	926	
Received, net	260	33	376	120	869	
Extended, net	202	47	119	135	57	
Short-term credits, net [4]	1 039	−52	608	272	9	
Overall balance	−2 175	−1 646	−282	−664	143	
Financing	2 175	1 646	282	664	−143	
Reserve assets	2 175	1 646	−490	−108	239	
Liabilities [5]	–	–	772	772	−382	

1. Including non-convertible currencies and transferable rubles: average exchange rate: 1990: 1Rbl=US$ 0.877; 1991Q1: US$ 0.992, April: US$ 0.586, May: US$ 0.561, June: US$ 0.574, July: US$ 0.565, Aug.: US$ 0.574, Sept.: US$ 0.577, Oct.: US$ 0.584, Nov.; US$ 0.225, Dec.: US$ 0.188.
2. No account taken of non-convertible currency transactions.
3. Includes travel, freight, insurance and investment.
4. Excludes transactions in 1991 to settle the outstanding liability position with IBEC; includes errors and omissions.
5. Includes net IMF loans and US$ 250 million in bridge financing from the BIS that should be considered an advance on the US$ 1 billion in G-24 exceptional financing; US$ 244 million was repaid in early 1992.
Source: National Bank of Romania.

the G24 and the EC.[9] A substantial fall in international reserves occurred at the end of 1992 and early 1993.

External financing of the balance of payments has been a binding constraint on the economy. Just how binding the constraint has been was illustrated in early 1992 when the failure of 800 million dollars of promised G24 financial assistance to arrive on time provoked serious economic difficulties. Attempts to mobilise domestic foreign exchange holdings for emergency imports, through the mandatory full surrender of foreign currency held by enterprises, were not successful and served to perpetuate chaotic conditions as enterprises sought to protect their earnings by not repatriating them. Financing problems emerged once again at the end of 1992 and early 1993 following a period when the exchange rate had been fixed without regard to the accumulation of reserves; the bunching of energy imports for the winter and delays in disbursements resulted in the almost complete exhaustion of international reserves.

The improvement in the current account for 1991 was driven entirely by the disintegration of the rouble trade in which Romania had been running a substantial deficit. Aggregate exports continued to decline but imports collapsed, particularly of energy and investment goods.[10] The convertible currency deficit improved as imports fell slightly and hard currency exports stabilized. An important factor limiting the fall in imports was the higher price of energy and the shift during 1990 of CMEA energy trade to convertible currency.

Figure 5. **THE COMPOSITION OF CONVERTIBLE CURRENCY EXPORTS**

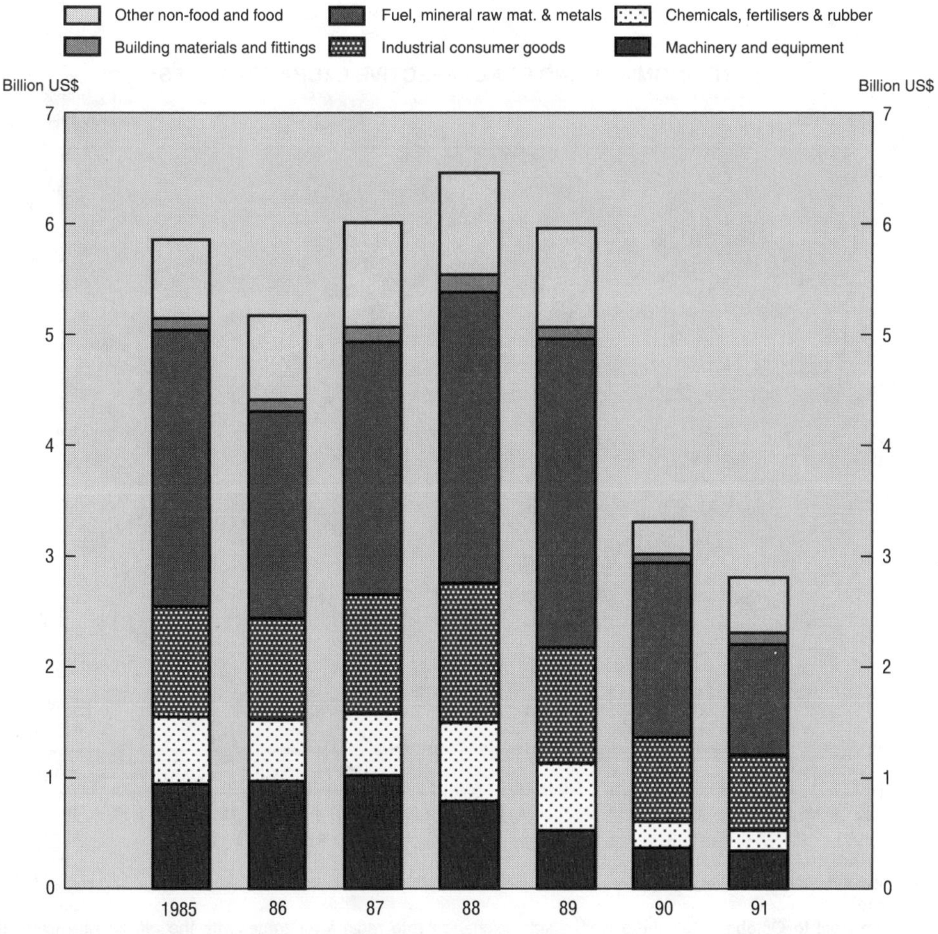

N. B. Breakdown is into "broad economic categories", not SITC categories.
Source: National Commission for Statistics.

The current account improved marginally in 1992 with the most notable development being the growth of exports. The improved export performance was driven by traditional, energy-intensive exports such as fertilisers and organic chemicals rather than in areas which were once important for Romania such as clothing, textiles and footwear. Imports remained subdued until the last quarter when energy and food imports for the winter surged. The time profile of imports reflects to a considerable extent government decisions and the enormous political concern to avoid the disruptions to supply during the winter as had occurred in 1991.

Although a structural analysis of the factors determining trade flows is extremely difficult, there are nevertheless indications that microeconomic rigidities have played a significant role in accounting for the development of trade flows in 1991-1992. Despite falling domestic demand, significant trade liberalisation and a substantial real depreciation in the first quarter of 1991 (Figure 6), neither exports nor imports responded as might

Figure 6. **NOMINAL AND REAL EFFECTIVE EXCHANGE RATES**[1]

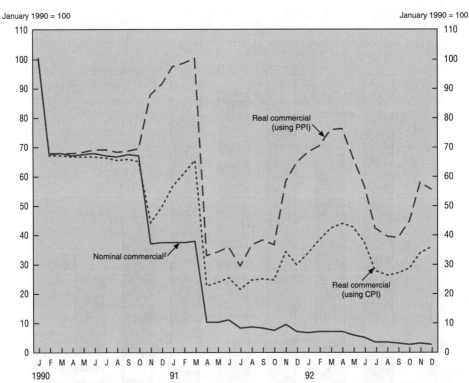

1. In the absence of reliable trade weights, the effective exchange rate has been calculated as (0.7 ECU + 0.3 US$) per lei.
2. From April to October 1991 there was a split exchange rate regime for trade, with the official rate fixed at 60 lei/US$ and a floating market rate. The two rates have been combined using approximate trade weights of 0.46 and 0.54, respectively.
Sources: National Bank of Romania, National Commission for Statistics, OECD statistics and OECD calculations.

have been expected. Exports did increase in line with the real depreciation in 1992 but the corresponding fall in imports appeared only to be temporary, imports picking up strongly in the last quarter. The lack of a clear relationship between movements in the measured real exchange rate and trade flows may be attributed in part to the fact that throughout this period the foreign exchange market was not in equilibrium and prices were often controlled. Administrative allocation of foreign exchange significantly influenced both the composition and destination of imports. Access to imported raw materials, in turn, may have played a more important role than relative prices in determining export capacities. While trade liberalisation surely opened up new trading possibilities at the margin, export controls on goods in short supply on the domestic market limited flexibility, and those importers who had to rely on foreign exchange auctions incurred both high risks and high costs.

The financial condition of enterprises

Information on enterprise profitability is not available for 1990 but over the period 1991-1992 it appears that the ratio of "profits" to sales declined gradually from around 5 per cent to 3.6 per cent in late 1992.[11] At the same time, enterprise cash flow deteriorated, as evidenced by the continual tendency for inter-enterprise arrears to build up. In the first nine months of 1990 there was certainly a dramatic fall in enterprise profitability. As against fixed prices for goods, production fell by 20 per cent while the wage fund increased by 11 per cent. During this period losses appear to have been around 38 billion lei representing 10 per cent of GDP.[12] The price reforms in November 1990 appear to have restored profitability to around the 5 per cent level observed in early 1991.

Although profit margins are comparatively low there are grounds for supposing that the true situation is much worse. Romanian enterprises have in aggregate been accumulating stocks, but the practice of writing off unsaleable inventories (i.e. valuing at the lower of market or historical cost) is not established – quite the contrary. At times, as in early 1991 and again in 1992, inventories have been administratively revalued to reflect inflation and the gains partially added to profits (see Chapter IV for details.) These were in addition to the "normal" inventory gains which arose as inventories were gradually revalued on the basis of historical cost under conditions of continuing inflation (Annex I). In terms of corporate cash flow, the decline in real profits has been offset by the elimination of most investment expenditures, the build-up of inter-enterprise credit, the partial write-off of enterprise debts to the banking system, and negative real interest rates.

The evolution of profitability took place against the background of slow labour adjustment and increased energy prices which, at first sight, should have led to a much greater squeeze on profitability. From its peak in the second quarter of 1990, average employment declined 17 per cent by mid-1992 (Figure 7). Over the same period, industrial production fell by some 50 per cent and GDP by over 30 per cent indicating a substantial increase in labour hoarding. Unemployment rose gradually throughout 1991 to 3 per cent, but accelerated during 1992, reaching 8.3 per cent by the end of the year. The comparatively slow adjustment of employment has been facilitated by real wage developments (Figure 8). The wage policy introduced in 1991 partially indexed wages to consumer prices. The surge in producer prices in November 1990, which was not immediately reflected in consumer prices, led to a halving of the producer real wage.

Figure 7. **THE DEVELOPMENT OF EMPLOYMENT AND UNEMPLOYMENT**

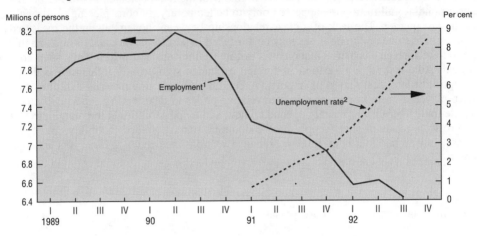

1. Average total employment; state, co-operative and mixed sectors; quarterly figures do not take into account seasonal workers, persons working on commission, persons working abroad or self-employed persons.
2. Quarterly average of mid-month unemployment rates; series unavailable before 1991Q1.
Source: National Commission for Statistics.

Figure 8. **CONSUMER AND PRODUCER REAL WAGES**

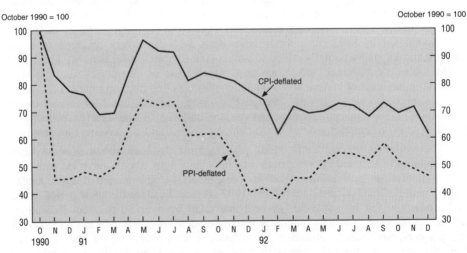

N. B. Average earnings in industry increased from 2 930 lei per month in January 1990 to 3 348 in October 1990 (14 per cent). There is no series for the CPI from January-September 1990.
Sources: National Commission for Statistics and OECD calculations.

Table 4. **The evolution of real energy prices to industry** [1]

October 1990 = 100

		Q1	Q2	Q3	Q4
Gasoline	1990				1.6
	1991	1.6	1.3	1.8	1.7
	1992	1.7	1.5	1.4	1.5
Natural gas	1990				1.3
	1991	1.2	0.9	0.8	0.7
	1992	0.7	0.6	0.6	0.7
Diesel fuel	1990				1.8
	1991	1.8	1.5	1.8	2.1
	1992	1.9	1.6	1.5	1.7
Heavy oil	1990				0.9
	1991	0.8	0.7	0.7	0.8
	1992	0.8	0.8	0.7	0.9
Crude oil	1990				1.5
	1991	1.5	1.3	1.1	1.4
	1992	1.4	1.3	1.2	1.4
Electricity	1990				0.8
	1991	0.8	0.9	0.8	1.4
	1992	1.3	1.2	1.1	1.2

1. The ratio of energy prices to the producer price index.
Source: National Commission for Statistics.

Although this was reversed to some extent in the second quarter, real producer wages remained on a declining path until the end of the second quarter of 1992. Since then controls on producer prices have resulted in a rebound of the real producer wage by some 50 per cent. Combined with an increased attention on the part of enterprises if not to minimum profitability, then at least to cash flow, this development may partly explain the acceleration in unemployment in the second half of 1992, when it rose by 3 percentage points.

Like all other CEECs, Romania pursued a policy of low energy prices in the past so that a major plank of the reform programme has been a policy of gradual adjustment to world energy prices. *A priori* this could have been expected to have had a major impact on enterprise profitability. However, the energy price shock appears to have been quite diffuse. While the real price of some energy sources rose by 90 per cent over the period, for others such as heavy oil and natural gas it appears to have decreased. What is surprising is the limited nature of the energy price shock in comparison to other CEECs, where it has been on the order of several hundred per cent.

Factors influencing the sustained decline in output

An important feature of the Romanian experience has been the depth and duration of the decline in output: indeed a decline in output was evident in the two years prior to the

Revolution, while other CEECs were still experiencing some growth. Moreover, this decline has taken place against an express policy objective of defending living standards and of seeking to break the fall in production. Within Romania there is surprising agreement on the proximate causes for the decline but divergent opinions on the role of policy. The output decline, it is argued, is related to the dependence of energy-intensive Romanian industry on imported energy and raw materials for maintaining exports and domestic production. The move to world prices in 1990 and 1991, in addition to other external shocks[13] decreased the capacity of the economy to import essential energy and raw materials. At the same time, domestic energy production fell for a number of socio-economic reasons. In combination these factors represented a proximate cause for the reduction of output. The most visible evidence for this process, it is argued, is the continuing shortage of these materials.

Although the pace and nature of structural reforms have been attributed a role in the decline (with divergent views on the speed of price liberalisation in particular), most attention within Romania has been focused on the stabilization programme. On the one hand, there is a view that credit conditions have been too tight, especially in 1992, leading to a fall in output greater than was needed. Moreover, the policy of high interest rates introduced in May 1992 is argued to be both inflationary and contractionary, reducing investment and aggregate demand. On the other hand, the unsustainable conditions that emerged following the expansion of nominal demand in 1990 is argued to show the ineffectiveness, if not the danger, of demand expansion. In this view, which seems analytically more defensible, a tight monetary policy was necessary not only to control inflation but also in view of the desperate foreign exchange situation. The high interest rates in 1992 were necessary not only to encourage holdings of lei deposits (which have as a result increased) but also to encourage firms to be more economising in their holdings of inventories and use of credit. The policy may have a greater output cost than usual due to the poor price/output split but, it is argued, this is unavoidable until firms adjust their behaviour to market conditions.

There is a great deal of truth to the claim that the energy intensity of the economy has been a major factor underlying the decline in output. The ratio of primary energy consumption to GDP was five times higher than in OECD Europe and at least double that of other CEECs: 1.9 tons oil equivalent/ GDP as against 0.4 in Europe and 0.78 in Poland.[14] Moreover, the elasticity of energy consumption with respect to GDP has historically been around 1.5. A large proportion of energy requirements were imported: by the end of 1989, domestic production satisfied only 60 per cent of domestic consumption. During 1990, supply disruptions[15] led to a drop in domestic energy production by around 20 per cent while the move to world prices, in combination with surging aggregate demand, lessened the capacity to import: the volume of energy imports fell by 15 per cent. As a consequence, domestic energy consumption declined by 12 per cent (consumption by households increased), explaining in an accounting sense the fall in industrial production and GDP. The decline in domestic energy consumption was more pronounced in 1991 as was the decrease in the volume of energy imports by some 44 per cent. Although domestic energy production recovered towards the end of 1991, the winter of 1991/1992 was marked by severe shortages of imports; in April only about 28 per cent of energy imports envisaged for the first four months of the year had been acquired.[16] The arrival of promised balance of payments support eventually permitted increased imports, foreign exchange being administratively allocated for this purpose. At the end of 1992 and early 1993, foreign exchange reserves fell dramatically in the wake of delayed energy and raw material imports while domestic energy stocks were reported to be nearly exhausted.

Although the energy-intensive nature of the economy – its dependence on energy-based exports and imported primary energy and raw materials – was a fundamental factor in the output decline, the duration and degree of the fall were heavily determined by the economic policies pursued. In this respect the stabilization programme *per se* is probably a less important factor than the approach taken toward structural policy. Romania faced a binding balance of payments constraint which required that foreign exchange, and energy imports in particular, be efficiently allocated. This did not occur because administrative allocation based on historical usage was maintained, including firms producing for inventories. A direct consequence of this approach has been a relatively modest change in the industrial composition since 1990 (Table 5). Industry is the dominant user of energy, accounting for as much as two-thirds of domestic consumption[17] but within the sector usage is highly concentrated: ferrous metals, oil refining and chemicals accounted for 55 per cent of energy used by industry in 1992 but for only a third of its gross output. Although the decline in industrial-sector output has become more differentiated by branch over the period, the level of uniformity is striking: energy-intensive industries have not declined by as much as could have been expected if energy and foreign exchange had been allocated efficiently.

The following chapters examine in more detail the ways in which structural policy has indeed been an important factor in explaining the poor macro-economic performance. At the same time they also assess the progress which has been made in creating the basis

Figure 9. **ENERGY PROFILE**

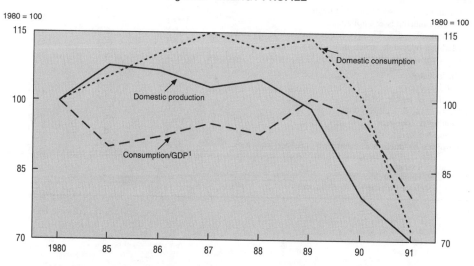

1. GDP in 1981 prices.
Sources: National Commission for Statistics, OECD calculations.

for a market economy and for a sustained recovery. This seeming paradox arises because structural reforms have been partial, and therefore often offset either by the lack of complementary reforms, or by policy actions running counter to the reform that were invoked as attempts to deal with immediate difficulties.

Table 5. **Industrial production by subsector**

Monthly average 1989 = 100

	1990	1991	1992
TOTAL INDUSTRY [1]	76.3	58.9	51.5
Energy production & extraction			
Coal mining & preparation [2]	59.6	49.7	65.7
Petroleum & gas extraction	87.9	75.1	72.0
Iron ore mining & prep.	66.6	51.4	55.4
Other extractive activities	91.9	68.5	52.5
Production & distribution of electric & thermic power, gas & hot water	75.9	63.2	59.1
Heavy industry			
Oil processing	76.7	49.2	43.6
Chemical industry & synthetic or artificial fibres	77.7	57.1	45.2
Rubber & plastics processing	72.2	52.1	42.2
Other products of non-metallic minerals	62.3	48.1	39.6
Metallurgy	72.3	51.5	40.6
Metallic constructions & metal products	61.9	51.6	41.8
Machines & equipment	89.2	58.1	52.5
Road transport equipment	74.5	56.1	46.1
Other transport equipment	70.4	52.5	51.9
Other			
Computers & associated equipment	73.0	44.9	37.8
Electric machines & appliances	100.2	71.0	54.5
Equipment, radio, TV sets & communication apparatus	66.3	58.7	44.5
Medical, optical & watch instruments & apparatus	65.7	53.2	45.7
Pulp, paper & cardboard	70.1	48.3	37.0
Light industry			
Food & drinks	80.8	65.4	59.9
Textiles & textile fabrics	77.4	64.5	51.7
Fabrics, fur & leather goods	73.6	65.4	52.1
Leather & footwear	80.3	67.4	55.3
Wood working	73.5	56.2	51.2
Furniture production & other non-classified activities	87.4	82.4	77.6

1. Unadjusted series.
2. Including bituminous shales.
Source: National Commission for Statistics.

III. Structural Reform in Enterprises

After two years of market-oriented reforms, a number of economic characteristics from the days of central planning persist. Industrial firms continue to face limited supplies of some key raw materials and energy products; importation of these items are constrained by the shortage of foreign exchange. In agriculture, the past three years have witnessed repeated government-declared crises in wheat harvesting and planting, requiring emergency allocations of inputs and credits to meet the demands of the autumn campaign. A few essential food items, like milk, remain difficult to find, and through late 1992 many other consumer goods remained in short supply – however, shortages of such goods appear to have largely disappeared in the course of 1992.

At the same time, new pathologies have developed. In apparent contradiction to the problem of shortages, industrial inventories have risen substantially since 1989, and anecdotal evidence indicates that the same is happening in agriculture with private grain inventories. *Pari passu,* there seems to be chronic illiquidity among firms: inter-enterprise arrears and financial ''blockage'' became a major problem in 1991 and have reappeared in 1992.

This chapter examines these phenomena in the context of an economy which is still in transition. It shows how the government's strategy of ''gradual reform at a fast pace'' has manifested itself in the speed and design of structural reform. It describes how the government's role in the economy has evolved, and the economic institutions which have resulted. The first section characterises the underlying philosophy of the Romanian reforms, some aspects of the state and the legislative and regulatory processes as well as the basic legal framework itself. The sebcond part recounts developments in the enterprise sector. The focus is on the incentives and constraints which govern the behaviour of economic agents, together with the price, allocation and external trading environment in which they operate. The same questions for agriculture – a core sector of the Romanian economy – are taken up in Annex II.

The legal and regulatory framework

The initial framework for reform in Romania, developed in 1990, was entirely home-made, reflecting the lagged effects of the country's estrangement from Western contact. The framework was provided in a seminal plan for reform begun in February and completed in April 1990,[18] followed by a series of white papers and reports by the Prime Minister which emerged later. It emphasised a commitment to market reform, and an increase in living standards for the population. The initial stage of reform was to focus on the development of private ownership reform, the reduction of the role of the state in resource allocation, and on the development of social protection. It was to be completed by June 1992.[19]

At the time of the reform's initial design, Romanian policymakers believed that if a gradualist approach were pursued, market reform could be consistent with little or no loss in income and with minimal social costs of transition. Thus the pace was to be gradual, or more precisely "gradual reform at a fast pace". Social protection was to be ensured through direct allocation, subsidies, a social safety net, and the indexing of wages for price developments. The state would continue to play an essential role in the allocation of key consumer and producer goods, especially the allocation of essential raw materials and scarce products,[20] with this role to diminish gradually over time.[21] Price liberalisation would proceed at different paces for different goods, depending on their importance in the economy. Lacking was any discussion of the coherence between the different speed of reform in allocation and in ownership.

The first priority of the reform process was an accelerated introduction of the legal and economic mechanisms strictly necessary for the functioning of a market economy. In doing this, Romania started virtually from scratch in creating the institutions to support a market economy, including the legislative process itself. The process faced political, philosophical and organisational problems. Of 90 laws submitted to Parliament between June 1990 and February 1991, only half were passed during that time period – still a significant accomplishment.

Romania created new institutions to strengthen public administration. A Minister of State (of Deputy Prime Minister rank) on Relations with Parliament was appointed with the sole responsibility of elaborating and co-ordinating a detailed legislative plan. A Council for Reform was formed consisting, *inter alia,* of legal specialists and economists to assist the government in the drafting, interpretation and implementation of laws, including design of appropriate institutions. Nevertheless, drafting of policy is still hampered by a lack of intra-governmental information flows and internal co-ordination has been weak. New policy proposals have rarely been discussed, analysed or negotiated amongst experts of different ministries before presentation to the Cabinet: this appears to have improved recently. As a result, key aspects of policy reform such as sequencing, implementation, institution building and financing have often not been fully examined.

The approach to legislation has reflected a legacy from the past: the underlying view that everything which is not permitted is forbidden. To illustrate, a law had to be passed permitting workers to hold more than one job. In addition to stifling initiative and innovation, this philosophy has overloaded the legislative apparatus, requiring laws on a multitude of minutiae, and making the formulation of coherent policy difficult. On top of the vast amount of legislation needed, many regulatory decisions are held up while awaiting government approval. Often the intent of legislation is undercut by regulation which is excessively centralised and bureaucratic, or the initial implementation is entrusted to bureaucratic interests opposed to its intent (*e.g.* the creation of private firms discussed below). While these problems are usually eventually resolved under pressure from economic agents, this iterative approach means that the rules of the game remain quite fluid, creating uncertainty.

The basic legal framework for a market economy was established over the course of 1990 and 1991, and was largely codified in the new Constitution, approved on 21 November 1991. Title 2 guarantees private property rights, regardless of owner, and forbids uncompensated expropriations. Title 4 defines Romania's economy as a market one and directs the state to ensure free trade and protect competition. However, accompanying provisions state that the content and limitations of these rights are established by law, leaving wide room for the Parliament to restrict them. Within this framework, legislation now provides many of the rules governing the entry and exit from economic activities and for institutions to support efficient market exchange, though there are many gaps.[22]

Mixed progress has been made in creating factor markets. Capital markets do not yet exist – their presence is largely moot until privatisation is further advanced. Planning has begun to create a stock market with the help of foreign technical assistance and it is expected to begin operation in 1993. The government has recently begun to issue negotiable debt instruments to the public bearing market rates of interest. For the private sector, the legal framework is in place covering the various forms of corporate governance: incorporation, limited liability, general and limited partnerships. Labour mobility and collective bargaining rights have been established,[23] but mobility is limited in practice because of lack of housing. A market in land is in theory permissible but, again, limited in practice; this is discussed in detail in the agriculture annex.

The framework governing market exchange and exit from economic activities is still deficient. The commercial code in use dates from 1887 (it was revised in 1938 but the earlier code was never repealed); work on a revision has just begun. A series of laws and decrees have been passed addressing bankruptcy and the collection of receivables, but an actual bankruptcy law is still pending: an old one is still *de jure* in effect but not enforced. A contract law exists but there is little practical experience with decentralised business decisions, and effective enforcement by the courts will be lacking for some time to come.[24] Anecdotal evidence suggests that in Romania, as elsewhere in the CEECs, contracts are not viewed as binding but as negotiable statements of intent,[25] while at the same time very literal interpretations of written agreements are common. In the areas of contracts and bankruptcy, enforcement remains as much a question of incentives and institutional practice as it is a legal one.

Structural reform and the enterprise sector

Building a market economy requires the creation of property rights and this requires action along three broad fronts: establishing governance structures for enterprises, imposing financial discipline on them so as to create proper incentives, and the liberalisation of price formation and resource allocation. In addition, it has proved essential in other CEECs to open foreign trade possibilities so as to relax the restriction that domestic supply and demand for individual products should balance, as well as to encourage rational price formation through competition. After reviewing developments in these areas, their influence both individually and collectively on enterprise performance is assessed.

Corporate governance

Corporate governance defines the incentives under which firms operate. In a market economy, direct private ownership and control frequently provide the incentives for profit maximisation[26] and cost minimisation; where ownership and control are divided, as is usually the case in large firms, such incentives are achieved through explicit contracts for managers, by monitoring on the part of financial institutions which have a debt or equity relationship with the firm, or both. To create corporate governance, the Romanian authorities have pursued a multi-pronged approach: the rapid privatisation of small state firms in services and trade; decentralisation of state enterprises, to be followed by privatisation; encouraging the emergence of new private firms; and facilitating foreign direct investment.

Governance of large state enterprises was addressed in August 1990 with the passage of Law 15 which sought to clarify managerial responsibility and decentralise decision making. State-owned enterprises were divided into two groups: those which would remain the property of the state for some time *régies autonomes*, (RAs) and commercial companies with state capital (CCs) which are eventually to be privatised. RAs were to be located in strategic industries and natural monopolies, (defence, fuels, mining, public utilities) and remain closely allied with the relevant ministry. The interrelationships between RAs and the relevant Ministry are however complex: in many sectors the Ministry appears to represent the interest of the RA (regulatory capture) while at the same time the RA is used as an instrument of government policy. Financially, RAs are part of the budget and are legally required to make a profit, unless losses are approved by the Government. They are eligible for state funding of investment and entitled to subsidies to cover losses. These latter conditions encouraged a number of firms to successfully lobby for RA status in 1990, stretching the definition of strategic industries and natural monopolies and increasing the potential demand on the budget. There are around 800 RAs,[27] of which nineteen are under central government control, accounting for 47 per cent of the nominal value of industrial assets. In 1992, recognising that the number and economic scope covered by RAs was excessive, the Government forced many of them to divest themselves of activities not in their main line of business. About 30 new commercial companies have been created to date from this process, and this will continue, coupled with the introduction of bidding-granted management contracts.

At the end of 1992 there were about 6 280 CCs, of which about 1 600 are in industry. These were formally removed from direct state "control" with responsibility given to managers who comprise a Board of Administration. The managers are accountable to a seven-member Council of State Representatives (reduced to three members in July 1992) appointed by the founding ministry and to which they are required to report. These councils usually include a representative of management, the trade unions, and the relevant ministry.

In principle, management of CCs has autonomy over daily decision making, while Councils have full autonomy to approve management operating decisions. Strategic decisions (*e.g.* closure of plants or of a division) have to be approved by the Council and then by the owners.[28] In practice, firms appear to be largely divorced from government control – there is neither a system for replacing council appointees nor of ensuring accountability. In turn, Boards of Administration are largely independent from the Councils so that enterprises are effectively autonomous, to wit "agents without principals".[29] A number of sources indicate that enterprise managements are now dominated by labour union appointees (as many as 70 per cent of enterprise directors were replaced with appointees of trade unions after the Revolution), so that the dominant management objectives might be maintaining employment and wages, within the ceilings created by wage indexation and the excess wage tax.[30]

The first step toward facilitating the founding and operation of private non-agricultural enterprises was in March 1990 with Decree 54. Under this decree employment in private firms was limited to 20 individuals and certain activities were banned. The Ministry of National Economy was empowered to sell raw materials, spare parts and other inputs to private enterprises, but subject to availability. In the following months, 140 000 requests for permits to open private business were submitted of which 80 000, mainly for retail activities, were approved by the end of the year.

Ambivalence on the part of some segments of the bureaucracy towards the private sector was still strong in 1990, with many bureaucratic practices and regulations undercutting the intent of new legislation. The Ministry of Resources and Industry issued instructions prohibiting any sole producer from supplying a private enterprise which, given the highly monopolised raw materials sector, was a serious threat. The Ministries of Agriculture and Health were reported to have forbidden all their units from concluding contracts with private enterprises.[31] Government Decision 201, which was passed in the summer of 1990, aimed at "... protecting the population against illegal commercial activities and at preventing private enterprises, in their attempt to get rich quickly without producing anything of their own, from destabilizing retail trade by acquiring for resale various types of goods, especially from the food sector, which goods should be made available to consumers through the state commercial network at state imposed retail prices".[32] "Drastic penalties" were imposed to enforce the law. By October 1990 (*i.e.* the first price liberalisation) only about 10 per cent of the individuals who had received permits in the preceding months had begun their activities.

This situation began to change in 1991 with the "small privatisation" of state assets in retail trade and services. Starting in November 1990,[33] the leasing (and sometimes sale) of state-owned assets has been pursued while at the same time the founding of private companies and partnerships was simplified.[34] As of mid-1991, 12 000 small-scale commercial units had been transferred to private administration (though not ownership) through franchise contracts; by May 1992 there were 19 664 such contracts. The franchises typically run for two years after which a full transfer of ownership is usually envisaged. The Privatisation Law enacted in August 1991 and the accompanying regulation seeks to simplify and accelerate the procedures.

By the end of 1992 new start-up firms and privately administered units translated into 200 000 private commercial companies in operation, accounting for around 1.4 million workers.[35] The private sector, including agriculture, accounted for over one quarter of GDP, up from 21.5 per cent in 1991, and 45 per cent of retail trade turnover – more than double the 1991 level (Table 6). The sector remains highly concentrated in services and trade and is characterised by very small-scale operations. The lack of capital markets makes capitalisation dependent on individual accumulation and partnerships, putting capital-intensive industrial activities largely out of reach of domestic interests. While this is certainly to be expected at this early stage of transition, there are still a number of other barriers to private sector development which prevent the sector from contributing more forcefully to the development of an efficient market economy. A survey conducted by the National Agency for Privatisation[36] (NAP) in the period November 1991-January 1992 pointed to three major barriers effective in that period:

Table 6. **The development of the non-agricultural private sector**

	Sept. 1991	Dec. 1991	Dec. 1992
Number of units			
Family associations (Law 54/90)	142 963	154 472	196 306
(operating), *of which:*			
– in trade			130 000[1]
Commercial companies (31/91) with private capital,	52 230	76 277	199 900
of which:			
– wholly or partly foreign-owned	6 104	6 433	21 056
– nominal value of equity (mn US$)[2]	200	267	543.6
Co-operatives		2 674	
Size structure of employment			
< 5 wage earners		31 931	
5-20		16 573	
21-50		9 281	
51-100		350	
> 100		60	
Total private-sector employment in:			
– non-agricultural (mn)			1.4[1,3]
– in agriculture (mn)			2.2[1,3]
Sectoral distribution of private companies (per cent)			
Production		15	
Trade		36	
Services		35	
Other		14	
Share of private sector in:			
Retail outlets			90
Trade turnover			45
Exports		19	26
Imports		18	32

1. Through September.
2. The actual value of the foreign direct investment could be substantially higher than the registered equity participation.
3. Interview with Mr. Severin, National Agency for Privatisation, "Nine O'Clock News", Bucharest, 1992. Other government
   sources point to private-sector employment of a little over one million.
Sources: National Agency for Privatisation, National Commission for Statistics.

- lack of access to raw materials, business supplies and equipment due to the refusal of state-owned suppliers to honour contracts, lack of allocation, and discriminatory pricing;
- widespread "corruption" (usually in the form of favours and presents) in obtaining materials and premises and in complying with expensive and time-consuming legal requirements;
- severe difficulty in obtaining premises and equipment.

The Romanian privatisation programme aims to privatise all 6 280 commercial companies (CCs) covering every sector of the economy, including agriculture, within seven years; *régies autonomes* are not to be privatised. This target was set forth in legislation approved by the Parliament, after much debate, in August 1991. To date, privatisation has largely been confined to retail trade and services (discussed above) and farming (discussed in Annex II). For other sectors, privatisation has been limited to some small pilot programmes. The main programme will only become operational in the course of 1993. This programme will be administered through six new institutions – five private Ownership Funds (POFs) and a State Ownership Fund (SOF) – which will acquire ownership of the enterprises and also responsibility for their sale.[37] Certificates of owner-ship (COs) representing some 30 per cent of the value of the assets – issued to the public at a nominal fee to cover distribution costs – will play an important role. Annex III contains a discussion of the mass privatisation programme scheduled to begin in 1993. It describes the institutional framework which has been established, and some of the potential risks faced by the programme as it assumes its final form and is implemented. This section describes the results of the privatisation programme till the end of 1992.

The Privatisation Law specified a programme for 1992 of ''early privatisation'' and ''asset sales'' which was carried out by the NAP. Early privatisation represented a pilot programme to sell some 30 companies, some through public offering, which were chosen for their good financial results. Proceeds of these sales were to be used to provide capital to the SOF and the POFs as well as to stimulate interest in privatisation more generally. The programme was, however, delayed with the first two sales only occurring in August 1992.[38] By the end of March 1993, eighteen enterprises had been sold.

Asset sales, by which is meant sale of activities, are to be a permanent feature of the privatisation programme.[39] For the 1992 programme, assets to be sold had to meet two criteria: they had to be physically separable operations, and their cumulative value had to be less than 75 per cent of the firm's social capital (roughly equivalent to shareholder's funds). Proceeds could only be applied to investment or to repaying loans. Companies were requested to nominate assets they wished to sell: around 5 600 sale offers were received from state enterprises involving employment of around 36 000. Very few of these offers were for industrial assets, suggesting the desire of enterprises to hold onto all existing activities. Through March 1993, 6 198 sale offers had been received for assets involving total employment of 41 799. Of these, only 1 846 transactions had been completed, involving employment of around 9 333 workers (Table 7).

During 1992, assets were sold by auction with the buyer under an obligation to keep the unit in operation for at least a year and not to lay off any workers for six months without compensation. The auctions were supervised by the NAP which was also respon-sible for verifying evaluations and establishing the initial bidding price; lack of specialists in this area proved an important barrier to a faster pace of sales. All bidders (foreigners were excluded in the first round[40]) were subject to screening according to explicit criteria designed to exclude bidders lacking the intention or the competence to carry on the business. Employees, both workers and local managers, could bid by putting 10 per cent down and receive a five-year loan at the savings rate for the remainder. If the asset was already leased, the present lessee had preference. Land titles have not as yet been sold, but new owners will have the right to buy land at prices determined by negotiation. The modalities established in 1992 are expected to continue in the future although the

Table 7. **The privatisation of state-owned assets**

	June 1991	December 1992	March 1993
Sale of companies (number)		15	18
Leasing of assets (number)	12 000		(Nov. 92) 25 286
– employees			110 030
– number in trade and tourism			15 538
Value of assets (bn lei)			182.5
Assets proposed for sale (number)		6 105	6 198
– in trade		2 976	2 996
– in tourism		1 711	1 753
– in industry		526	536
Employment in assets proposed for sale		41 268	41 799
– in trade		5 942	5 954
– in tourism		11 890	12 078
– in industry		12 974	13 216
Assets sold (number)		1 514	1 846
– in trade and tourism		1 259	1 547
– employees		7 967	9 333
Distributed certificates of ownership (mn)		15.5	

Source: National Agency for Privatisation.

Ownership Funds will take over the role of the NAP and vouchers may be available as a source of funds.

Even at this early stage, rather unspecific allegations of spontaneous privatisation have arisen. By spontaneous privatisation could be meant the sale at nominal prices of plant and equipment to private businesses controlled by friends or relatives of enterprise managers, or asset sales to these persons. Managers are prevented from participating in the usual auctions for asset sales. It is difficult to judge how widespread these activities have become. Spontaneous privatisation may increase the speed at which some enterprises are privatised, but unless it is made more transparent there is the risk of a political backlash against the whole programme.

Foreign direct investment

Foreign investment presents another method of creating private enterprise. It has been permitted since March 1990. Through October of that year, only 567 applications had been received, mainly small, of which 362 were approved (with the remainder in process). Throughout 1990, majority control by foreigners was not permitted and repatriation of profits in foreign exchange was possible only up to a sum representing 8 per cent of the initial contribution of foreign capital to the firm.[41]

A substantially more liberal regulatory framework was instituted in April 1991. The new law ensures national treatment for foreign firms: it provides for open access to nearly all sectors, limits the grounds on which applications may be rejected, and permits 100 per cent foreign ownership of Romanian firms. Several financial incentives for investment which are still operative were included: six-month to five-year tax holidays depending on the sector; reduction in profit taxes, dependent on the reinvestment of profits;[42] and reductions for two years in customs duties on imports of energy, raw materials and capital equipment. In mid-1992, changes to foreign exchange regulations eliminated restrictions on the repatriation of dividends. (Profits from convertible currency operation can be repatriated without limit subject to 10 per cent withholding tax). However, one restriction remains important: the Romanian constitution prohibits foreigners from acquiring land. An amendment to the foreign investment law passed both chambers of Parliament in March 1993 clarifying the right of all Romanian juridical persons, including those with foreign ownership, to own land, but as of this writing was held up by a parliamentary committee. The number of firms with foreign participation jumped in 1991 and 1992 (Table 6) although most remain quite small. The outstanding stock of foreign direct investment stood at about 600 million dollars by the end of 1992.[43] The low level appears to be attributable to the high level of uncertainty concerning macroeconomic stabilization and the exchange rate: in value terms a large proportion of investment to date is in the areas of trade, agriculture, foodstuffs, banking and energy exploration. For the latter, payment is to be taken in the form of buy-backs of energy products.

Financial reform and financial discipline

In a market economy financial institutions serve to impose budget constraints on firms, to monitor enterprise governance, to allocate capital efficiently, and to transmit monetary policy impulses to the economy. Under the centrally planned economy, finance performed none of these roles, and operated in a strictly accommodative manner. In Romania this situation continued during the first year after the Revolution. The decentralisation of firm decision making was accompanied by a financial policy wherein banks[44] were instructed to extend credit to enterprises to meet higher labour costs. Later in the year, the credit plan, which was approved by the government, included requirements to clear domestic payment arrears, to cover losses from previous years and to finance existing stocks.[45]

During 1991 and 1992, the banking system was restructured in order to establish monetary control and to bring enterprises under increased financial discipline. In December 1990, the Romanian financial system became a two-tier banking system with the National Bank of Romania (NBR) spinning-off all its commercial activities to the newly formed Romanian Commercial Bank (RCB) and limiting itself to the functions of a central bank.[46] The RCB and other state-owned banks all became commercial companies with the freedom to negotiate financing contracts with enterprises for the implementation of investment projects. The sectorial specialisation of banks was abolished. In April 1991 new banking and central bank laws were passed which established the principle of universal banking and made banks responsible for their lending operations.

The change in legislation has not yet created a system which can effectively monitor firms or allocate financial resources based on market criteria. The connection between savings and lending is still tenuous, as these functions are largely performed by different institutions. The Romanian Savings Bank (CEC) dominates the deposit market. It a has network of 2 300 branches and 26 million accounts giving it over 60 per cent of total deposits. The CEC accounts for less than 5 per cent of direct loans to customers. The remainder of the bank's assets are lent directly to the NBR or the RCB at floating interest rates for periods of 10 years. The RCB alone makes 35 per cent of customer loans, with the Foreign Trade Bank and the Agricultural Bank accounting for most of the remainder. The spread between deposit and lending rates has not yet become a market-determined relationship.[47] Though the new banking law liberalised interest rates on all liabilities (subject to regulation), this has had a limited effect on deposit rates. The CEC accounting system is so antiquated (much of it is still handled through handwritten ledgers), that the bank is technically incapable of changing deposit rates more than twice per annum, making it difficult to adjust to changing rates of inflation. Financial efficiency is further impeded by delays in check clearing on average, 6.7 working days, which implies a financial transactions tax of around 2 per cent.

Under the old regime, banks had little role in allocating credit. Banks accounted for only 10 per cent of investment finance, the rest coming from the budget or retained earnings. The new banking law permits banks to lend up to 20 per cent of a bank's capital to an individual firm,[48] but many banks have inherited levels well above this. Anecdotal sources indicate that banks remain under pressure to lend to meet wage payments of large state enterprises. While a number of technical assistance programs are in progress, bank management and staff lack the experience and technical training to adequately perform credit evaluation, which is in any case difficult under conditions of partial price liberalisation and macroeconomic instability.

The government has attempted to prevent debts inherited from the old regime from impeding the normal functioning of the financial system. In a bid to clean up both bank and firm balance sheets, many outstanding bank debts of enterprises were cancelled. At the end of 1989, loans to the enterprise sector amounted to 683 billion lei. During 1990, a total of 280 billion lei[49] of unserviceable enterprise debts (about one-third of 1990 GDP) were written off against accumulated government budget deposits. Another 125 billion lei of doubtful debts were at first refinanced by the NBR but not written off. At the end of 1991, a further 155 billion lei of bad debts incurred before the Revolution and in the course of 1990 were cancelled, 135 billion lei replaced by government liabilities and the remainder charged to the banks. In addition there have been several rounds dealing with old investment credits, with the government providing guarantees. At the end of 1991, several state-owned banks had negative capital and most were highly under-capitalised. Estimates suggested that around 200 billion lei would be necessary to recapitalise banks so as to comply with the standard BIS 8 per cent capital/asset ratio. In mid-1992 a bank recapitalisation committee was formed and an injection of 69 billion lei was made from the budget's foreign asset revaluation account at the NBR.[50] Not all old non-performing debts have been settled (although inflation has reduced the significance of old relative to new debt), and the banks remained under-capitalised at the end of 1992.[51]

Despite the write-off of bank loans to enterprises, tight monetary policy in the first three quarters of 1991 was accompanied by an explosion of inter-enterprise arrears and the increasing illiquidity of firms (Chapter IV). Arrears began to appear in early 1991, and by September they were estimated to have exceeded the value of bank credits to enterprises. These growing arrears were seen as threatening the imminent breakdown of the production system through non-payment of inter-enterprise credit. In response, in December 1991, the Parliament passed the Law on Settlement of Outstanding Payments (Law 80). This Law instructed the NBR to address the arrears problem and clear the "blockage" of payments. This was accomplished by a generalised extension of credit (global compensation credits) through the banking system of 400 billion lei net (the gross amount of arrears was 1.8 trillion lei).[52] Enterprises were required to use these credits to pay suppliers in successive rounds of settlement which were largely completed by the end of February 1992 so that arrears were largely eliminated. However, by mid-1992 the problem had once again emerged, with gross inter-enterprise arrears equivalent to about 20 per cent of GDP. Inter-enterprise arrears stabilized over the third quarter of 1992 as a result of the injection of low-interest credits by the NBR, especially 40 billion lei to the energy sector, a principal source of payments blockages. Arrears began to accelerate again in the fourth quarter and by year end 1992 had reached about 30 percent of GDP. These have again served to severely disrupt the economy.[53]

Recent studies by the government and outside consultants indicate that arrears are highly concentrated. One hundred twelve firms in three industrial branches – mechanical engineering, chemicals, and metallurgy – account for 55 per cent of total arrears. These same firms consume 40 per cent of total energy and raw materials, but account for only 15 per cent of value-added. The list of firms is currently under review to determine whether the financial condition of some enterprises on the list may result from price distortions rather than fundamental factors. The government has adopted a new three-part program to deal with the arrears problem more generally. First, it has extended 100 billion lei in selected credits (terms of three months at 25 per cent interest) to firms which, according to strict selection criteria, should be assured to repay them. Second, it plans to financially isolate the main offenders from the banking and enterprise sector, preventing further creation of arrears. Third, it will require that interest, above market levels, be charged on arrears by all enterprises.

Price and trade liberalisation

Prices in a market economy serve to equilibrate supply and demand, preventing shortages. For firms, relatively high (low) prices and associated profits (losses) serve as signals encouraging (discouraging) the allocation of resources to sectors most needing to expand (contract). These elements are reinforced by trade liberalisation which allow imports and exports to equilibrate markets and provide competition for domestic producers, and the importation of world relative prices on which to base resource allocation and comparative advantage. Further reinforcement, especially in non-traded goods sectors, is typically provided by carefully crafted and effectively enforced competition statutes.

The creation of these conditions in Romania was envisaged as a gradual, staged process. The first stage took place in November 1990.[54] The price reform "liberalised" all final goods prices with the exception of forty basic consumer goods, whose prices were left unchanged. Prices for 77 basic raw materials used in industry, whether of domestic or imported origin, were not liberalised. For all but twenty of these commodities, prices were raised in line with the devaluation (i.e. by 75 per cent: from 21 to 35 lei/dollar), although prices to industry for energy were increased further. The remaining twenty remained fixed at pre-devaluation levels.

The November 1990 price reform established a pattern which has been maintained through subsequent stages in April 1991, July 1991 and in a series of steps in the course of 1992. The prices of different categories of goods were liberalised at different speeds: some were permitted to be determined freely in the market, some were raised and refixed to reflect "world market prices" (in line with exchange rate devaluations), and a few remained fixed and controlled at previous levels. Over the course of two years, the general pattern appears that the prices of those goods which were the most important in the production or consumption basket were liberalised most slowly.[55]

Simple description of price reform is complicated by numerous regulations which cross over the categories of prices which have been liberalised and those which remain controlled. These additional regulations cover prices in monopolistic sectors, essential consumer goods, and "products for which there is a significant demand-supply disequilibrium".[56] For products and services for which there do not exist more than three suppliers, prices are set by "negotiation with the economic agents" under close government supervision. In practice, the process of negotiation does not search for a price to equilibrate demand and supply. Rather, producers are expected to justify the prices they propose on the basis of accounting costs and "legitimate" mark-ups. In 1992, 15 per cent of all goods were said to be in this category, accounting for around 40 per cent of turnover. For other goods, a mark-up ceiling of 30 per cent was established in retail trade to control speculative profits arising under conditions of shortage; if the margin is exceeded, fines can result. Putting these two categories together, in late 1992 around 60-70 per cent of turnover was subject to price controls or price supervision exercised by the Ministry of Finance and Economy.

Central planning by the government through the use of material balances was completely eliminated in Romania in 1990. However, administrative allocation of some raw materials by the Ministry of Industry continues,[57] though the number of items has continually declined. During 1990 and 1991, 400 raw materials for which there was excess demand at current prices were so allocated. Practically all of these goods were also "monopoly goods" subjected to price controls. This number was reduced to 33 in January 1992, and to ten items in late 1992. These goods are mostly energy and energy-related product (*e.g.* natural gas, oil, and refined oil products). It appears that direct allocation is declining in comprehensiveness as well as scope – trade liberalisation means that firms are permitted to import these items directly, subject to access to sufficient foreign exchange.

A second round of price reform occurred in April 1991 and was accompanied by the introduction of a dual exchange rate system (see Chapter IV for details). An important objective was to reduce producer subsidies which in part arose from the November price reform.[58] Controls on food prices were lifted except for ceilings on twelve basic food groups. Controlled prices on 88 imported raw materials and energy products were raised in line with the devaluation, but were set on the basis of the official rate of 60 lei/dollar rather than at the much higher market rate of around 180 lei/dollar. While oil prices were brought into line with "world levels", electricity and gas prices remained well below marginal import costs – domestic gas prices were at 50 per cent of world levels.

A third round of price reform occurred in July 1991, liberalising more consumer goods and some raw materials prices. Only fourteen consumer categories (five food and nine services, as well as industrial energy prices) were still subject to price controls. Thus by the third quarter of 1991, the share of "free" prices in the total value of sales had risen to 83 per cent for consumer products, 88 per cent for capital and intermediate goods, and 70 per cent for raw and basic materials. During the course of 1991, central allocation became less effective because some materials were directly imported (a direct consequence of trade liberalisation – see below) and demand for them fell in line with the general collapse of output.

Prices were increased again, though not liberalised, with the unification and devaluation of the official exchange rate in November 1991. The government also issued Decision 776, which attempted to stabilize producer prices. The decree set limits on some prices and all margins, and required that price increases be announced 90 days in advance. With the exception of the latter requirement, it in many ways formalised what had been practice throughout 1991. Decision 801 required all producers to report negotiated prices to the Ministry of Finance; the same rule applied to the prices and margins charge by importers. The authorities allowed several months for the effects of the November depreciation to pass through into prices, and then refixed them in February-March 1992. Official prices for energy and raw materials were set on the basis of an exchange rate of 180 lei/dollar.[59] Many of these goods are subject to central allocation as discussed above.

In April 1992, prices for oil, electricity, coal and lignite were raised to world levels, and natural gas prices were raised by 300 per cent to 55 per cent of import prices from the CIS.[60] World prices were, however, calculated at the price-fixing exchange rate. An interesting feature of the move to world market prices is that prices to industry appear to have been only marginally affected (Table 4).

After May 1992, the exchange rate began to depreciate bringing raw material and energy users into acute difficulties. Enterprises which imported raw materials at the higher market rate of exchange remained confined to pricing at the lower price-setting rate.[61] By August it was clear that the system was on the verge of collapse: since February producer prices had changed very little as a consequence of fixed raw material prices, Decision 776, and the rules on monopoly pricing described above, while the exchange rate had depreciated by over 100 per cent. This was addressed by Decision 312 which increased the price-setting exchange rate to 360 lei/dollar[62] and reduced the pre-notification period to 30 days. It appears that Decision 312 does not introduce real price flexibility into the system of setting producer prices. At the time of writing, price changes were permeating through the system, both for controlled prices and for negotiated and supervised prices, with prices being set according to the prevailing exchange rate of the day. The result has been that different prices in the economy are set according to widely varying exchange rates, having the same *de facto* effect on domestic prices as a multiple exchange rate system. Press reports indicate that producers which were able to do so were pricing as high as 800 lei/dollar, based on exchange rates paid by acquiring foreign exchange on the unofficial market. The government has responded by declaring that pricing imports at these levels is illegal and will be prosecuted. A commodities exchange was instituted in autumn 1992 to help provide more complete markets; a special decision was needed to exempt commodities contracts from price control regulations.

In September 1992 retail price controls were completely eliminated on sugar and meat. The government was several months behind in supplying these commodities at subsidised prices, so that production was still "owed" to the population. In theory this leaves only the prices of bread and milk controlled; in practice it appears that prices on many consumer items, at least in state-owned retail outlets, are now subject to supervision based on strict mark-up limits, so that many prices are still not market-determined. Simultaneously with the elimination of all consumer subsidies, direct controls on all consumer prices are expected to be totally removed in May 1993.

Trade liberalisation

Following the Revolution, the government moved quickly to liberalise trade: quantitative import restrictions were lifted and the state foreign trade monopoly was abolished in February 1990.[63] As an interim measure, in January 1990 tariffs were reduced and rationalised. New rules for export and import licenses were also introduced; import licenses were issued almost automatically in 1990. However, a kind of import restriction has been maintained *de facto* through the various schemes for rationing foreign exchange; because of this, import competition has in fact been limited. In addition, import licences are still required for goods under quotas such as sugar, and numerous reports continue to circulate that such licensing is restricted or subject to corruption.

Since the lifting of most explicit quantitative restrictions on imports in 1990, the tariff has become the main formal instrument of commercial policy. A tariff code which was in compliance with the GATT[64] was put in place in January 1991 with the object of introducing competition into the economy and improving incentives.[65] Tariffs were lowered in September 1991 to an average level of 12 per cent following the introduction of a basic tariff schedule (Table 8). A waiver from their GATT obligations was requested in December 1991 and has been extended until 30 June 1993. However, for reasons which may have been connected with a desire to hold down inflation in the opening months of 1992, the new schedule was replaced by a temporary one for 1992 with an average tariff of around 5 per cent (Table 8). The reduction was achieved by a substantial increase in the number of exempt tariff lines although the temporary schedule includes tariff quotas (*i.e.* after the quota is exceeded the tariff increases to the basic rate). Adding to policy activism, in May 1992 temporary surcharges of 30 per cent were imposed on 23 goods comprising around 7 per cent of imports,[66] which were scheduled to lapse on 1 January 1993.

Export prohibitions and quotas have been maintained on goods in short supply or subsidised by the budget, ranging from sugar and wheat to furniture. By the end of 1992, a number of quantitative restrictions on exports, many of them introduced in 1991, were still in force. The number of export quotas was reduced from 112 to 33 commodities in January 1992, and again in May 1992 to 22. Quotas are allocated on a first-come, first-served basis. Export prohibitions were cut from 81 to 36 categories, and in mid-1992 to 19; ten are food items and the remainder are basic materials such as wood, all of which

Table 8. **The structure of the Romanian customs tariff, 1992**

Tariff rate	Basic	Temporary for 1992
	Number of tariff lines[1]	
Exempt	62	783
1-5 %	322	1 085
6-10 %	959	1 174
11-15 %	969	472
16-20 %	1 278	421
21-25 %	925	679
26-30 %	450	353
31-35 %	5	5
> 35 %	49	46
Total	5 018	5 018
Average weighted tariff [2]	12	5

1. Based on the harmonised system.
2. Government calculations.
Source: Ministry of Trade and Tourism.

are considered in short supply. The intention is that quotas and prohibitions will be eventually eliminated, except for subsidised consumer goods.

Romanian exporters face a number of barriers to exports to the OECD area in the form of voluntary export restraints (VERs). In 1989, only nine of the top 100 Romanian product categories to the OECD area encountered no non-tariff measures (NTMs) although two important exports, furniture and glass products, encountered relatively few NTMs.[67] In 1992, VERS covered agricultural goods and textiles (EC, Sweden, Norway, Canada, United States) while Germany and Italy maintained restrictions on steel imports. Moves to normalise Romania's trade regime with the OECD area have been delayed by political developments in Romania. Thus it was only in 1992 that Romania received most-favoured nation status from the EC while this was rejected by the United States Congress in 1992. Negotiations for an Association Agreement with the EC were completed in late 1992 and signed in early 1993. An agreement with EFTA was signed in early 1993.

Competition policy

Competition policy as understood in the OECD does not yet exist in Romania, with the exception of provisions regarding the breaking up of state enterprises under the Transformation Law.[68] Laws and regulations concerning competition generally try to constrain "speculative excess" and "profiteering". An example of this is the Law on Unfair Competition (11/1991), which regulates behaviour and unfair practices. Its provisions prohibit employing the employee of a competitor, entering into contracts on discount terms with the intention of adversely affecting competition, or selling a product which attempts to pass itself off as the product of a competitor.[69]

The government has drafted a new competition law which has been presented to Parliament. If previous draft Romanian competition statutes are any guide, there is considerable danger that the present draft may not give sufficient independence to the office charged with implementing the law. Just as serious, the proposed law may contain a good deal more price control power than is found in traditional market economy competition statutes. However, under the terms of Romania's association agreement with the EC, trade between the two will be governed by competition provisions. The draft competition law conforms to the provisions of the Community.

Assessment

Corporate governance and financial discipline are still very much in transition in Romania. Industrial firms have been decentralised but not privatised. Some, especially RAs, are still subject to direct and indirect state control, but the majority are constrained by neither plan nor owners, living in a behavioural twilight, apparently strongly influenced by labour union objectives. In services and trade, a growing private sector has emerged, but is constrained by its intermediary role, dependence on the state sector, and limited access to foreign exchange. Foreign investment has had little impact.

The financial system is not being used to compensate for the lack of direct corporate governance: banks neither impose hard budget constraints nor monitor firm performance, and are as yet incapable of allocating credit along market guidelines. The lack of corporate governance and financial discipline has resulted in the build-up of inventories, financed by bank credit and inter-enterprise arrears. Progress on passing a bankruptcy law remains important, but will remain mere window-dressing without effective enforcement and incentives for agents to use it.

One-time write-offs of enterprise debts are initially appropriate to remove uneconomic, non-performing loans inherited from the centrally planned economy, but when repeated simply reinforce the message of financial laxity.[70] In Romania, the cancellation has been drawn out over the last three years leading to the creation of conditions encouraging moral hazard. In particular, there was an incentive to blur the cut-off between old and new debts: many firms have justified application for debt forgiveness on the grounds that they were due to losses incurred through price controls and therefore outside their control (*i.e.* they belonged to the "old system").

Through 1992 the response of the Romanian government to the build-up of inter-enterprise arrears has dealt with only the symptoms – financial blockage – but not the cause – financial indiscipline. Repeated injections of credit – first the global compensation scheme of December 1991 and then the partial compensation scheme of August 1992 – represented yet another reason for firms to believe that they were not operating in a monetary economy. This approach has undermined monetary credibility and further distorted the rules of the game away from the introduction of a market economy.

The new government's March 1993 strategic reform plan includes several forceful measures to deal with financial indiscipline and arrears: passage of a bankruptcy law, introduction of mandatory interest payments on inter-enterprises credit, financial isolation of persistent loss-making firms from other firms and the banking sector, creation of a unit to restructure or close these firms, and another injection of credit to healthy firms to clear arrears. While these measures present a clear commitment to enforcing greater financial discipline, difficulties are likely to be encountered in their implementation. On the one hand, relative price distortions and arrears themselves make it difficult to determine the true financial state of enterprises. On the other hand, the programme is likely to encounter stiff opposition from state enterprise managers and trade unions, as well as certain ministries within the government. It remains to be seen whether, and if so how rapidly, these reforms will be implemented.

A characteristic of the Romanian economy has been the persistent propensity for stockbuilding. The obvious factor permitting the accumulation of inventories has been the lack of financial discipline on firms, which has allowed inter-enterprise credit to grow; low to negative real rates of interest have also been a facilitating factor. But other factors have contributed and may have even been causal: continued stock accumulation is not counted as a cost under Romanian accounting standards, so that profits have been maintained by production rather than sales. It is hardly surprising that firms have become increasingly illiquid and the tendency to increase overdue inter-enterprise credits irresistible.[71]

The gradual, staged approach to price reform has not resulted in true price liberalisation. Instead, many prices are still set, and reset, in line with world market prices, and even liberalised prices are, in many key sectors, closely supervised and based on strict control of margins. Price controls and price monitoring have been accompanied by continued, though decreasing, administrative allocation of key raw materials. In a period of high and variable inflation, with repeated devaluations, this changing mix of fixed, negotiated and liberalised prices has meant that relative prices have been highly unstable. Producer prices have tended to jump at each devaluation, followed by a period of catch-

Figure 10. **CHANGES IN RELATIVE PRICES IN INDUSTRY**

Monthly percentage
growth rate over period

Monthly percentage
growth rate over period

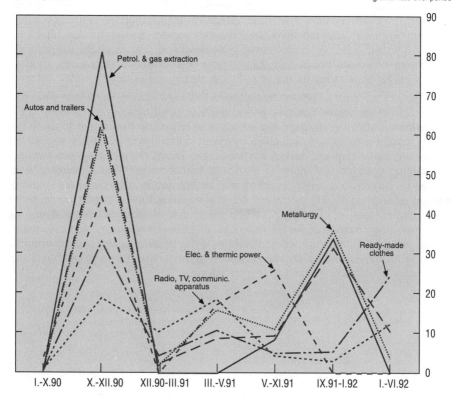

Sources: National Commission for Statistics and OECD calculations.

up by consumer prices. Amongst producer prices, relative prices have been highly variable conveying little information to direct resource allocation. Prices serve neither to allocate resources efficiently nor to clear markets, while prohibiting firms facing chronic excess demand to earn sufficient profits to expand capacity.

Direct allocation of resources has been accompanied by "government failure." In 1990, instead of closing the most inefficient plants, physical allocation simply scaled back the output of most plants in heavy industry by 30-40 per cent, thus effecting limited economies of energy and raw materials, while keeping employment of these factories virtually untouched. This pattern has generally continued in 1991 and 1992 even though more targeting has been introduced; allocation rights still favour the continuation of production and, therefore, of "needs".

Despite warnings as early as 1990 from the World Bank,[72] the government, with its preoccupation with smoothing the transition and protecting incomes, chose to maintain differential speeds of price liberalisation, and ignored the possibility that partial liberal-isation could interact with other reforms to produce pathological outcomes. This is what happened. The combination of partial liberalisation, continued direct allocation and lack of hard budget constraints inhibited a positive supply response. Not surprisingly, the repeated devaluations have had little effect on reallocation of resources within the economy in favour of competitive, traded-goods sectors. Rather, limited adjustment has created a vicious cycle of depreciation, price shocks to raw materials, the gradual pass-through to consumer goods and wages, little reallocation of resources, shortages of foreign exchange, and finally the need for another round of devaluation.

The gradual pace of reform has allowed those with the most to lose – bureaucratic elements from the central-planning period and their constituencies – to retain some power and influence, affecting the pace and substance of reform. In the current situation the state administration is weak, having given up direct control over economic agents. Interest groups are well-organised, and in key instances control the means of production while maintaining symbiotic relations to particular bureaucracies. These interests have suc-ceeded in perpetuating some direct state interventions in the economy, inhibiting the nascent reliance on market incentives, while at the same time acting to vitiate, subvert or delay implementation of reforms. While the extent of these activities should not be overstated, they have contributed to a lack of policy consistency and coherence, and helped undermine domestic policy credibility by generating charges of government cor-ruption and cronyism. This has created doubts in the minds of foreign observers as to the government's true commitment to market reform.

IV. Macroeconomic Policy

The government's principal policy goal in 1990 was to revive the living standards of the population after the harsh repression of the Ceausescu years. Policy measures were intended to redirect resources towards consumers: nominal wages were increased in the face of fixed prices, and work hours were cut, especially in the energy field. A large monetary overhang constituted an additional source of demand pressures,[73] and was reinforced by substantial real growth in monetary aggregates. The financing needs of state enterprises were accommodated even as demand for their investment goods fell and output went into inventories. As discussed in Chapter II, in the face of surging demand and the structural mismatch of demand and supply, liberalisation of the foreign sector led to an explosion of the balance of payments deficit. The payments deficit swelled to around 9 per cent of GDP, financed entirely by the drawdown of foreign reserves. By October 1990 the black market premium on the exchange rate had risen to 500 per cent in the face of enormous repressed inflation, and exchange reserves were down to two weeks of import cover. In November, to relieve these pressures, the exchange rate was devalued and prices partially liberalised, while the government began to develop a macroeconomic stabilization programme.

The experience of 1990 demonstrated the need for stabilization to accompany structural reform and set the macroeconomic policy agenda for both 1991 and 1992:[74] stabilizing the price level after price liberalisation and achieving a viable balance of payments (including an increase in reserves), while at the same time sustaining real incomes. To achieve these goals, the stabilization programme was to be based on tight control of money and credit supply, supported by a small budget deficit and tax-based partial wage indexation. Programme goals for the exchange rate were less clear, other than the general goal of gradually moving towards foreign exchange convertibility on current account. Because of the lack of international reserves – part of the legacy of 1990 – the authorities recognised that the exchange rate could not serve as a nominal anchor. Nonetheless, subsequent behaviour indicates that the authorities did try to maintain a fixed rate for extended periods to help fight inflation. Perhaps because of these ambiguous policy goals, this practice was not accompanied by an interest rate policy designed to ensure an adequate build-up of international reserves and to establish confidence in the lei.

Intermediate targets of macroeconomic policy instruments have generally been met, but satisfactory macroeconomic performance has proved elusive (Table 9). This chapter reviews the course of macroeconomic policy in 1991 and 1992, focusing on the principal causes for this slippage. The first section reviews developments in monetary and exchange rate policy, highlighting the influence enterprise financial indiscipline and other

Table 9. **The stabilization programme: objectives and outcomes**

	1991	1992
	Objectives – (Outcomes)[1]	
GDP growth	0.0%	0.0%[2] (–15.4%)
Revised	–5.0% (–15.4%)	
Inflation		
Year-end	15.0% p.a.	1.5% per month
	(10.3% per month)	(9.6% per month)
Year-on-year		115%
Revised		150% (224%)
Average	120%	180%
Revised	163% (165.5%)	270% (210.4%)
Current account (bn US$)	–2.4 (–1.4)	
Reserves (mn US$)	–600 (–822)	500 (–200)[3]
	Macro instruments	
State deficit (% GDP)	2.4 (0.8)[4]	2.0 (4.0)
Broad money growth	15% (101%)	88% (75%)
Credit growth	20% (117%)	67% (34%)

1. Figures in parentheses are the outcomes.
2. The objective was to halt the fall in output. With the fall in output which occurred in 1991, if this had been achieved in early 1992, GDP would still have been 5 per cent lower in 1992 than in 1991.
3. Preliminary.
4. After settlement of inter-enterprise arrears in early 1992.
Sources: National Bank of Romania and OECD calculations.

structural distortions have had on policy outcomes. The evolution of exchange rate policy is given particular attention. The second section discusses fiscal policy. From a macroeconomic perspective, the central theme is that the budget has been balanced essentially by decapitalising declining state enterprises, while at the same time using off-budget funds and monetary policy to cover the burgeoning costs of financial indiscipline and price distortions. The chapter concludes with a brief discussion of wage policy.

Monetary and exchange rate policy

Objectives and conduct of monetary policy

The goal of monetary policy was to prevent price liberalisation from becoming embedded in inflation. To achieve this a tight monetary policy objective was adopted: the monetary overhang was to be sharply reduced and the velocity of money raised. The extent of the monetary overhang at the beginning of the reform period is extremely difficult to judge. The ratio of money supply to nominal GDP had been rising steadily since 1988, and jumped from just over 55 per cent at the end of 1989 to around 70 per cent in September 1990 (60 per cent for the year as a whole, see Figure 11). This surge was accompanied by clear indications of excess demand for consumer goods.

In 1991 the monetary targets were for growth of 15 per cent and 22 per cent in money and credit, respectively. The inflation rate was expected to decline over the year to an annual rate of 15 per cent in December, while averaging 120 per cent for the year as a whole, implying a substantial contraction of the real money supply. In 1992 the same strategy was pursued: the policy targets for monetary and credit growth were 88 per cent and 67 per cent, respectively, against a projected increase in the price level of 115 per cent.[75]

Although the inflation assumptions underlying the programme were wide of the mark in both 1991 and 1992, the authorities have been successful in decreasing substantially the money/GDP ratio. In the face of considerably higher inflation than anticipated, monetary targets in 1991 were exceeded by a wide margin. Nevertheless, for 1991 as a whole the ratio declined from 60 to 50 per cent. In 1992, the inflation assumption was considerably higher than for 1991, implying increased targets for monetary growth. Although inflation turned out to be greater than projected, the monetary aggregates have been held to the authorities' original growth rate targets. The money/GDP ratio fell from 50 to 33 per cent in 1992. The velocity of circulation of broad money, 3.0, is now not greatly different from levels approached by countries with a similar per capita GDP, and is higher than historical levels in Romania.

In seeking to target the money supply, the authorities were initially hindered by a lack of policy instruments and therefore had to rely on control of domestic credit. With government financing and net foreign asset flows outside the direct control of the NBR,

Figure 11. **INDICATORS OF MONETARY OVERHANG:**
THE RATIO OF MONEY SUPPLY TO GDP

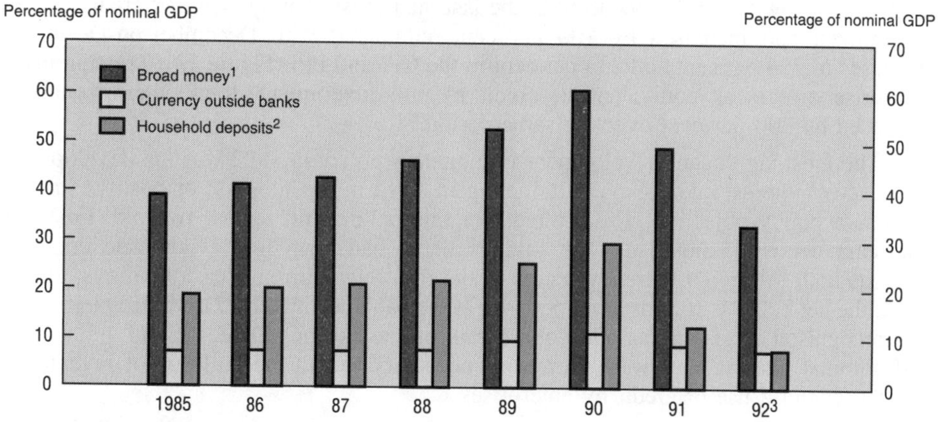

Percentage of nominal GDP

Percentage of nominal GDP

Broad money[1]
Currency outside banks
Household deposits[2]

1. Including foreign exchange deposits.
2. Time and demand deposits, in lei.
3. GDP subject to revision.
Sources: National Bank of Romania, National Commission for Statistics.

55

this has meant in practice seeking to control the volume of enterprise credit. From January to September 1991, individual bank credit ceilings were in force, supported by the NBR refinancing mechanism.

In 1991 interest rates were not used as an instrument of monetary policy and had no role in the allocation of capital. Interest rates were liberalised in April 1991 but the rigid nature of the banking system, the segmented credit market and the ceilings on the volume of individual bank credit prevented bank competition for deposits and the free negotiation of interest rates.[76] Throughout 1991, the savings bank (CEC), which effectively controls deposits, maintained interest rates at 6.25 per cent in the face of an annual inflation rate over 200 per cent. Banks borrowing funds from the CEC at about 10 per cent had to set low lending rates: the NBR maintained a 3 per cent limit on the spread between the cost of funds and the average lending rates. In the last quarter of 1991 the NBR refinancing rate was increased from 14 to 18 per cent but for short-term credits extended by commercial banks, the rates stayed in the range 11-16 per cent, rising in November to 12-22 per cent.[77] With open access to lending from the savings bank, the discount rate set by the NBR was largely irrelevant.

Monetary targets were strictly adhered to through September 1991, but then control lapsed in the last quarter (Figure 12). From the end of 1990 through September 1991 the growth of net domestic assets was only 6 per cent, with the growth of credit to the enterprise sector marginally higher. This implied a substantial contraction in real terms – the counterpart of the sought-after fall in real money balances.[78] Industrial production continued to plummet in the last quarter and enterprises began to accumulate arrears at an accelerating rate, doubling between September and December. Faced with fears of an imminent collapse of the payments system and of production, from October the individual bank credit ceilings were abolished and credit aggregates surged, culminating in December with the net injection of 400 billion lei as part of the global compensation scheme to clear inter-enterprise arrears (under Law 80; see Chapter III).[79] The injection of credit under the latter scheme did not represent a change in the policy of the NBR but was forced on it by the Parliament to which it is ultimately accountable. Three-quarters of total credit growth in 1991 occurred in the last quarter, so that by year end credit to non-government had increased by 100 per cent, compared with December-on-December increases of 224 per cent and 233 per cent in the CPI and PPI (Figure 13). Treating inter-enterprise arrears as equivalent to credit to non-government, total enterprise credit increased by 300 per cent over the same period.[80]

The most significant development in monetary policy in 1992 was the development of an active interest rate policy, culminating in April in the adoption of positive interest rates as a policy objective. The grounds for this policy shift appear twofold. First, the dominant deposit-taking bank, the savings bank, had been losing domestic currency deposits both to foreign currency accounts and to foreign currency cash holdings: during 1991, the net balance of household deposits at the bank declined by 21.5 billion lei.[81] This was recognised as placing an additional strain on the exchange rate. Second, higher real and nominal interest rates were viewed as necessary to halt the build-up of inventories and the wasteful use of credit by enterprises.

From January 1992, the CEC and other financial institutions were compelled to pay "market-related rates" (meaning in effect rates more related to the NBR's refinancing rate) on their negotiable instruments; the NBR lifted its refinancing rate from 18 to 28 per cent, initiating an increase of deposit rates to 17-28 per cent and short-term credits to 28-36 per cent. In April, following a difficult first quarter on the foreign exchange market

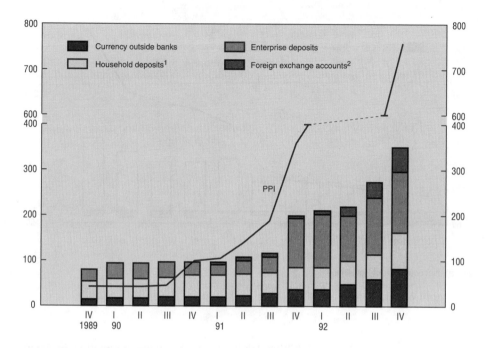

Figure 12. **STRUCTURE OF NOMINAL MONEY DEMAND**
End-of-period, December 1990 = 100

1. Time and demand deposits.
2. Time and demand deposits of households and enterprises.
Source: National Bank of Romania.

and in bank deposits, the government signalled its intention to pursue a policy of positive real interest rates with respect to anticipated inflation, although significant slippage has been apparent. The refinancing rate was raised at the end of May to 80 per cent with the rates on short term credits increasing from 28-36 per cent to 68-85 per cent and those on deposits from 17-28 per cent to 20-67 per cent.

During the first half of 1992 there was very little growth in monetary aggregates: credit to economic agents actually fell through June 1992, and broad money grew by only 5 per cent. As in 1991, this implied a considerable fall in real monetary and credit aggregates. In 1992 the NBR was concerned to sterilise the secondary effects of the increase in money supply following the settlement of inter-enterprise arrears in December. Minimum reserve requirements were introduced in March (10 per cent of deposits) to replace individual bank credit ceilings. This was accompanied by the first auctions of refinancing credit. While these measures were important, the substantial drop in credit growth was undoubtedly due to higher interest rates. But since inter-enterprise arrears were interest-free, the process of substituting such arrears for bank credit became even

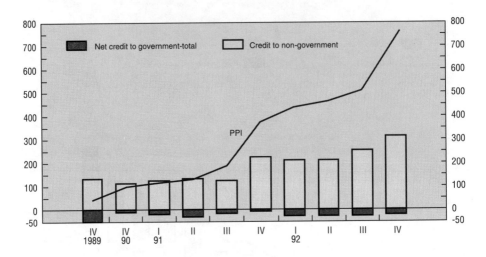

Figure 13. **STRUCTURE OF NOMINAL CREDIT**
End-of-period, December 1990 = 100

Source: National Bank of Romania.

more pronounced, reaching 1.2 billion lei by June after their elimination in January (Table 10).

With the re-emergence of arrears and financial blockage in the second quarter of 1992, monetary policy came under immediate political pressure to provide selective preferential credits at low interest rates. Beginning at the end of August, refinancing credits, at 13 per cent to support loans at 15 per cent, were provided to selected industries: 100 billion lei to agriculture, 40 billion lei to industry (mainly energy producers, as large industrial energy consumers are the main source of financial blockage), and 15 billion lei to exporters. Total outstanding refinancings averaged around 340 billion lei over the same period. This effectively stabilized inter-enterprise arrears at the June level through to September. Growth in the sum of inter-enterprise arrears and credit to non-government during the first three quarters was 150 per cent, compared with 132 per cent growth in the CPI and an estimated 65 per cent increase in the PPI. It appears that the government intends to continue the policy of low interest credits to certain sectors in order to ease the financial blockage. As part of an overall effort to resolve the financial blockage, the government announced in early 1993 up to 200 billion lei in three-month credits at 25 per cent interest.[82] Another 15 billion lei in low interest credits have been announced for agriculture, and 70 billion lei for exports. Romanian press accounts indicate that farmers are unwilling to utilise credits from an IBRD loan on the expectation of cheaper government credits.

Broad money and credit grew very strongly in the last quarter of 1992. Money growth had already accelerated in the third quarter – to around 6 per cent per month – and this strengthened through November. In December it may even have reached 20 per cent.

Table 10. **Inter-enterprise arrears, money, credit and industrial production**

	Broad money	Credit to non-government	Inter-entreprise arrears [1]	Index of industrial production [2]	PPI
	Billion lei			December 1990 = 100	
December 1990	514	684	100	100.0	100.0
January 1991	519	703	206	95.1	107.7
February	546	731	307	87.9	107.9
March	517	756	400	103.3	108.1
April	525	765	482	101.4	128.6
May	568	788	550	105.9	133.4
June	567	811	600	99.8	133.7
July	595	839	637	98.2	142.9
August	600	806	691	93.9	170.2
September	598	749	800	90.9	187.0
October	663	839	1 000	94.7	203.0
November	805	899	1 317	79.9	254.4
December	1 024	1 368	1 777 [3]	74.2	365.7
January 1992	1 066 [4]	1 312 [4]	– [4]	80.9	404.1
February	1 048	1 247	n.a.	84.4	415.0
March	1 085	1 270	n.a.	87.1	443.4
April	1 073	1 292	970	76.6	449.7
May	1 099	1 275	1 122 [5]	75.3	449.7
June	1 123	1 274	1 199	73.4	459.0
July	1 198	1 323	1 321	66.2	474.8
August	1 322	1 451	1 234	62.4	481.4
September	1 425	1 546	1 237	67.8	510.0
October	1 446	1 684	1 607	70.2	599.7
November	1 540	1 743		72.5	742.1
December	1 768	1 907		63.7	762.0

1. To December 1991, M. Khan and E. Clifton, "Inter-enterprise arrears in transforming economies: The case of Romania", IMF Paper PPAA/92/1, July 1992. 1992 information supplied by the Ministry of Finance. For 1992, arrears refer to credits overdue beyond the contract date, usually 30 days.
2. Unadjusted for number of working days.
3. The net enterprise arrears amounted to around 400 billion lei.
4. Includes the effect of the global compensation of December 1991.
5. In addition, 158 billion lei were in arrears to banks.
Sources: National Bank of Romania, National Commission for Statistics.

An important element of the expansion of the money supply has been the growth of foreign currency deposits of both households and firms (Figure 12). This has led to increased holdings of foreign currency by banks (there is no requirement to remit this to the NBR) and to excess bank liquidity. Higher interest rates also had an effect on the composition of the money supply. Overall deposits at the savings bank and other banks declined by 10 billion lei during the first four months of 1992 but increased by more than 36 billion lei during the period May to September 1992.

Exchange rate policy

At the time of the October 1990 price liberalisation, the exchange rate was devalued to 35 lei/dollar, more in order to attempt to maintain the competitiveness of existing exports[83] than to clear the exchange market, despite the fact that foreign exchange reserves had been virtually exhausted. At the same time, the free market exchange rate continued to show a discount of around 500 per cent; there was very little narrowing of the two rates.

Faced with a further deterioration of the convertible currency balance in the first quarter of 1991, the NBR introduced a dual exchange rate system in April 1991.[84] This reflected conflicting objectives: the necessity to adapt to a binding balance of payments constraint, the desire to minimise price adjustments and inflation and the wish to protect certain industries. The official rate was devalued to 60 lei/dollar and applied to a priority list of imports, essentially food, energy and raw materials. These commodities were subject to administrative allocation since their internal price was too low to eliminate shortages. Some reports indicate that as much as 80 per cent of imports were paid at the low official rate. Foreign exchange was made available by a 50 per cent surrender requirement (at the official rate) on all exports. All other transactions were conducted at a commercial rate, established through inter-bank auctions, which depreciated steadily throughout the year. The gap between the official and market rates thus increased (Figure 4). The exchange rate policy pursued throughout 1991 succeeded neither in rebuilding reserves nor in ensuring a supply of foreign exchange to meet demand at the official rate.

A major shift in foreign exchange policy occurred in November 1991 when the foreign exchange rate was unified at 180 lei/dollar 1991 – representing a depreciation for official uses but an appreciation with respect to the pre-existing commercial rate of around 300 lei/dollar. All domestic foreign currency accounts (around $500 million), except for those held by individuals and joint ventures, were compulsorily acquired by the government at the new exchange rate of 180 lei/dollar, and a 100 per cent surrender requirement was instituted for exporters. The immediate reason for the change in policy was the urgency to finance winter fuel imports, made worse by the failure of promised G24 support to arrive on time. A much more fundamental reason was the clear failure of the dual rate system.[85] The unification reduced but did not eliminate the spread between the free market and official exchange rates.

The foreign exchange regime instituted in November was also intended to be a move to internal convertibility implemented as a managed float. In fact in 1992 it became a system characterised by foreign currency rationing: at the official exchange rate there was substantial excess demand. One reason for the shortage was that the exchange rate was not permitted to affect relative prices: in order to control inflation and to influence wage negotiations, the effect of the depreciation was not allowed to pass through to prices for a period of up to three months and even longer (Chapter III). The shortage of foreign currency was compounded by enterprises holding export earnings in offshore accounts or not exporting at all given the effective appreciation of the real exchange rate for exporters. After the government exhausted the foreign reserves generated by the November mandatory full surrender, a severe foreign exchange shortage ensued. Petroleum imports were constrained resulting in electricity shortages. Institution of strict administrative controls forcing repatriation of export earnings supplied some foreign exchange, but probably resulted in further substantial under-invoicing. The NBR reported a queue of three to four months for approved foreign exchange applications to be filled. Not surprisingly the free market exchange rate continued to depreciate, falling by some 15 per cent in March alone.[86]

The severe difficulties encountered in the first quarter led to a series of measures extending over the period April to September which moved the system closer to convertibility. In April an interbank market was re-established and foreign exchange offices were allowed full access to this market. The surrender requirement was abolished altogether in June. At the same time, as noted above, interest rates were increased substantially. Finally, from June the authorities allowed a gradual depreciation of the official rate which fell from 223 lei/dollar in May to 430 lei/dollar in September. The market rate also depreciated over this period but by much less, so that in August the two rates effectively converged, and this was maintained through November.

By August the authorities appeared to have achieved their immediate goal: the real exchange rate had been devalued and exports had started to increase strongly. The interbank auction was functioning well despite the attempts of some banks to acquire foreign exchange for their own account. The negative side of the policy adjustment was that, as before, the exchange rate had not been allowed to feed through into prices: until September some raw materials and energy had been priced at an accounting rate of 180 lei/dollar, far below the official interbank rate. In September this was raised to 360 lei/dollar but by this time the official rate had reached 430 lei/dollar. Throughout the period increasing sums were paid as compensation to enterprises for this arrangement (see below). Expectations were built in that the rate would continue to depreciate until producer prices converged with the exchange rate. As a result economic agents continued to view foreign exchange as a superior store of value, and the volume of foreign currency offered continued be inadequate to satisfy demand.[87]

From September to December 1992, the NBR effectively "fixed" the official rate at 430 lei/dollar during the daily clearings. The grounds for this policy shift appeared to be the desire to hold exchange rates constant during the long process of re-negotiating administered prices and to maintain political and social stability for the period surrounding the October election, the oncoming winter, and government transition.[88] At the same time, the shortage of official foreign exchange reserves was already apparent. The authorities might have been misled into believing that the fixed rate was appropriate by developments in the foreign exchange market. In line with a trend observed in the preceding months, the daily value of transactions going through the market increased. Exporters appeared to be able to finance many of their own imports directly while foreign currency loans received by the government (such as the Structural Adjustment Loan from the World Bank) were directly allocated to enterprises for critical imports using the accounting exchange rate. Substantial excess demand at the fixed rate was nevertheless apparent although this did not translate immediately into a rise in the free market rate. One reason for this might be the increase in supply at this time following the mid-year surge in exports; domestic foreign currency deposits of enterprises and households continued to increase at the same time as inter-enterprise arrears mounted. Demand for foreign currency was driven by the low returns from holding lei assets in comparison to the high returns from holding foreign exchange: the ex-ante real interest rate was certainly still negative. Returns to foreign currency holdings were increased by factors such as the safety of foreign currency accounts from creditors and the ability to raise bank loans on the collateral of these accounts.

Towards the end of 1992 reserves fell strongly as winter imports surged, and were practically exhausted by the middle of January. At the same time, the delayed liberalisation of prices resulted in a steep increase in monthly inflation. Pressure on the exchange rate increased with the black market rate increasing from around 430 lei/dollar to around

800 lei/dollar by mid January. Interest rates were held constant. As a result the NBR let the official rate depreciate in stages, reaching 500 by the end of January.

Assessment

Determining the stance of monetary policy – the question of whether it was tight or accommodative – involves not only assessing the evolution of money and credit aggregates and interest rates, but also correctly identifying expectational factors including the degree of policy credibility. Money and credit may be viewed from both stock and flow perspectives. From the former perspective, customary aggregates indicate a tight stance: real money and credit fell strongly over the period. However, there are a number of difficulties with these measures. Real credit fell in part through substantial debt write-offs amounting to some 350 billion lei since 1990. Indeed the drop in nominal credit during the third quarter of 1991 was in part due to a write-off of old debts and enterprise losses (Chapter III) – a part of these were debited against idle government deposits. Whether the surplus government balances constituted potential transactions balances, and therefore contributed to inflation potential, is however questionable. In sum, monetary policy was tight although possibly overstated by traditional measures. As argued above, the sum of inter-enterprise arrears and credit may be a useful indicator of inflation potential. From this perspective, monetary conditions cannot be considered to have been tight – although this was only indirectly due to monetary policy. Viewed from the flow perspective the policy has been stop and go, damaging credibility. In the first half of both 1991 and 1992 it was tight, with the rate of growth of money being below the rate of inflation. In other periods, such as the last quarter of both 1991 and 1992, it has been expansionary.

The dramatic growth of inter-enterprise arrears in 1991, and again in 1992, has been taken as an indicator of excessively tight monetary policy but is actually a better indicator of structural distortions and the lack of an effective transmission mechanism. If inter-enterprise arrears had reflected the tightness of money and credit, then pressure on the market exchange rate should have lessened; in fact the opposite occurred. Rather, inter-enterprise arrears in Romania reflect stock-building of unwanted goods, losses, payments indiscipline and even the accumulation of foreign currency holdings: they reflect barriers to the effective implementation of monetary policy. Measures taken to write-off enterprise arrears, while not at the same time strengthening financial discipline, served to undermine attempts to tighten monetary policy. Under conditions of severe structural distortions the monetary aggregates may convey limited information in comparison to developments in financial markets.

Over most of the period interest rate policy has been to some extent at cross purposes with both the intermediate targets and final objectives of monetary policy. In 1991 interest rates were highly negative regardless of the deflator used, creating enormous incentives to borrow to build stocks and undermining the exchange rate. In the first half of 1992, this policy appears to have been reversed as interest rates were raised substantially by May. But whether real interest rates were in fact positive in the key *ex-ante* or expectational sense is difficult to ascertain. As a result of formal and informal price controls, discussed in Chapter III, producer price inflation was repressed to a level of 17 per cent at an annual rate between March and August 1992. With lending rates approaching 70 per cent, producers faced real interest rates approaching 50 per cent annually. Critics have focused on this figure. However with inflation clearly artificially suppressed, expected inflation may have been quite high – indeed the free market exchange rate gave indications of such expectations. Thus the *ex ante* real interest rate may have been quite low and even negative. Reinforcing the tendency to negative real interest rates was the introduction of increasing amounts of preferential credits.

The hope of positive real interest rates for savers proved brief and illusory. Over the period of March to August 1992, CPI inflation averaged 90 per cent at an annual rate, though there were signs that this was decelerating to under 50 per cent by July and August. Although deposit rates remained negative in real terms, the policy at least made them less so and, possibly as a result, savings accounts started to increase in the second and third quarters. However, with the exchange rate continually depreciating, the returns from holding foreign exchange were much greater leading to increased foreign currency holdings. With the availability of 15 per cent financing beginning in July, growing inter-enterprise arrears, repressed PPI inflation in the face of 100 per cent depreciation, and another (gradual) round of subsidy cuts and price decontrol due in September, it must have become clear to economic agents that inflation was likely to re-accelerate, further undermining the credibility of monetary policy.

Without structural reform an aggressive real interest rate policy which also targeted the exchange rate was probably not a viable option for the NBR. Drawn-out price reforms increased the uncertainty premium which would have driven nominal interest rates up still further. At the same time, poor financial discipline meant that the policy was ineffective. Even if inter-enterprise arrears had been kept under tight control, it is likely that interest capitalisation would have occurred since, in the end, there was no real possibility of enforcing bankruptcy on insolvent enterprises.

With regard to the exchange rate, the dominant conviction has been that without foreign exchange reserves or a stabilization fund, a stabilization of the lei (*i.e.* its use as a nominal anchor) was not possible. Exchange rate policy was nevertheless assigned the role of assisting the control of inflation by directly holding down the prices of imported raw materials and intermediate inputs – subject to the constraint that sufficient foreign exchange for essential imports would be generated. As a consequence, few policy initiatives were undertaken to make the lei more attractive to hold as an asset. Quite the contrary: a number of measures, some of which have already been discussed in Chapter III (*e.g.* safety of foreign exchange from creditors demands), have directly contributed to increasing returns from holding foreign exchange. Beginning in 1992 the additional goals of establishing internal convertibility on current account and rebuilding foreign exchange reserves were added – but subject as before to the goal of directly stabilizing inflation.

As a consequence of these somewhat contradictory policy objectives, the Romanian authorities have not sought to set the exchange rate at a market clearing level but rather control it administratively.[89] Foreign exchange regimes have been changed frequently with insufficient attention to credibility. Unsuccessful attempts to fix the rate have been repeatedly followed by sharp devaluations of the official exchange rate. This has been in contrast to the more measured development of the free market rate. Further, a direct result of trying to manage the exchange rate in the absence of market clearing has been that devaluations of the official exchange rate have repeatedly lagged the market exchange rate,[90] so that another devaluation was built in, validating expectations of depreciation and further undermining confidence. The result has been repeated devaluations and regime changes, a complete loss of confidence in the currency, and the frequent and continued resort to rationing in the allocation of foreign exchange.

Inflation and inflation expectations appear to be deeply embedded in the Romanian economy. The drawn-out nature of price reforms, by increasing uncertainty, has certainly been an important contributing factor. However, the primary factors include monetary conditions in general, and monetary policy in particular. The lack of financial discipline and the non-credible approach to clearing inter-enterprise arrears has undercut monetary policy, increasing the inflation potential for any given level of money supply. Monetary policy, through its stop-go nature and frequent recourse to preferential credits did not have the credibility to lead to revisions of inflation expectations. This was importantly reinforced by the inability to raise the price of money (*i.e.* to pursue an effective real interest rate policy). Taken together, the exchange rate has been under continual pressure leading to an unstable price/exchange rate dynamic. In sum, the policy outcomes were both a product and a cause of the macroeconomic conditions discussed in Chapter III, but an important contribution has also been made by shifting policy objectives and inconsistent policy settings.

Fiscal policy

Fiscal policy goals and outcomes

During 1990 the principal goals of fiscal policy were to diminish government size and its role in the economy, rather than macroeconomic policy targeting as such. Particular targets were to reduce the size of government in terms of employment and revenues, lower the tax burden, devolve investment spending onto state enterprises, and contain wage increases for direct state employees.

With the emergence of severe macroeconomic imbalances during 1990, the government tried in 1991 and 1992 to balance a goal of maintaining fiscal discipline with the provision of a social safety net, while at the same time keeping the share of budget expenditures and incomes in the economy on a downward path. The government set a target of 2.4 per cent of GDP for the state budget deficit[91] to support the monetary and balance of payments targets in the April 1991 macroeconomic stabilization programme. The 1992 goal was to maintain a state budget deficit of roughly the same size, around 2 per cent of GDP. An increase in the budgeted deficit above the 2-3 per cent range appears to be under consideration for 1993.

The general government budget was in substantial surplus under the old regime, reaching a peak of 8.4 per cent of GDP in 1989. These surpluses were the counterpart to the large trade surplus used for debt prepayment (the foreign debt repayment fund was an extra-budgetary expense). Despite the dramatic drop in GDP since then, the government has been able to maintain its goal of controlling the recorded fiscal deficit. The general government budget resulted in a small surplus in both 1990 and 1991 (Table 11), and a deficit of 1.1 per cent in 1992. In both 1991 and 1992, state budget deficits exceeded projections as expenditures, particularly on subsidies, accelerated with inflation. But in both years these deficits were offset by unanticipated surpluses in the extrabudgetary funds as unemployment was lower than forecast.

The satisfactory position of the budget through 1992 appears rather surprising in light of the dramatic declines in output. There are several reasons for this. First, the

Table 11. **General government budget**

Billion current lei

	Average 1985-88	1989	1990	1991	1992	Budget 1993[1]
Current revenue	406.5	407.9	338.5	790.3	2 130.0	
Tax revenue	267.3	264.9	307.3	778.1	2 069.0	
State and local taxes	218.9	211.0	244.3	502.0	1 302.1	2 315.7
Profit tax			62.2	110.3	315.7	
Tax on net production	76.8					
Excess wage tax	1.3	1.1	1.5	5.7	n.a.	
Wage tax (individual income)	46.0	50.1	58.0	166.8	457.7	
Custom duties	0.7	0.7	0.9	16.5	78.6	
Turnover taxes and excises	86.7	150.6	101.3	182.5	418.5	
Other[2]	7.5	8.5	20.4	20.2	31.6	
Funds, of which:	48.5	53.9	63	276.1	766.9	1 436.7
Social security contributions	40.8	44.3	53.3	164.0	468.8	768.5
Supplementary pension fund	7.6	9.6	9.7	22.0	74.5	49.6
Unemployment fund				35.4	136.8	225.5
Other funds[3]				54.7	86.8	393.1
Non-tax revenue and transfers	139.2	143.0	31.2	12.2	61.0	
Remittances from profits	82.0	88.7				
Capital revenue			2.7	6.3	n.a.	
TOTAL EXPENDITURE[4]	363.6	341.1	332.4	766.3	2 189.1	4 104.9
of which: state and local				596.3	1 826.4	2 741.9
Current expenditure	218.7	200.9	266.6	664.8	2 018.1	
of which:						
Goods and services[5,6]	140.5	120.4	107.1	285.3	726.5	
Transfers and subsidies	71.0	79.5	104.7	379.6	1 291.6	
Transfers	64.8	75.7	100.7	236.1	649.9	
From central budget				46.0	122.0	206.1
Social security outlays[6]	3.2	3.5	54.8	159.4	406.6	689.7
Unemployment fund				6.9	44.9	198.9
Supplementary pension fund				6.7	25.4	58.2
Other funds[7]				17.0	51.0	342.3
Subsidies[8]	6.2	3.8	4.0	142.6	635.2	
To enterprises[9]				52.8	105.7	
To the population				82.0	511.2	
To public institutions				7.8	18.3	
Interest payments	7.3	1.0		0.9	6.5	
Capital expenditure[10]	144.8	140.2	65.8	101.5	171.0	
OVERALL BALANCE	42.9	66.8	8.8	30.3	−58.7	−282.5

			(as % of GDP)			
TOTAL REVENUE	48.4	51.1	40.4	37.8	39.1	35.3
Tax revenue	31.8	33.2	36.4	36.9	38.0	
Non-tax revenue & transfers	16.6	17.9	3.7	0.6	1.1	
Capital revenue			0.3	0.3	n.a.	
TOTAL EXPENDITURE	43.3	42.7	39.4	36.3	40.2	37.9
Current expenditure	26.1	25.2	31.6	31.5	37.0	
Capital expenditure	17.3	17.6	7.8	4.8	3.1	
OVERALL BALANCE	5.1	8.4	1.0	1.4	−1.1	−2.6

Table 11. **General government budget** *(cont.)*

Billion current lei

	Average 1985-88	1989	1990	1991	1992	Budget 1993[1]
	(as % share)					
TOTAL REVENUE						
Tax revenue	65.8	64.9	90.1	97.7	97.1	
Non-tax revenue & transfers	34.2	35.1	9.1	1.5	2.9	
Capital revenue			0.8	0.8	0.0	
TOTAL EXPENDITURE						
Current expenditure	60.1	58.9	80.2	86.8	92.2	
Capital expenditure	39.9	41.1	19.8	13.2	7.8	
Memorandum item:						
GDP (billion lei)[11]	839.5	798.0	844.0	2 109.7	5 450.0	10 830.0

1. Projected
2. 28.9 billion lei included for estimated 1992 local budget tax revenues.
3. 1991: includes research, health, export promotion and selling houses funds; 1992: includes research, health and education funds. 1993: also includes accident and risk fund for disabled persons, special social security fund for agricultural labour force and other funds.
4. Net of transfers to local government in 1991 and 1992.
5. Including health fund.
6. Prior to 1991 social security outlays are included in goods and services.
7. 1991: research and export promotion funds; 1992: research and education funds. 1993: also includes accident and risk fund for disabled persons, special social security fund for agricultural labour force and other funds.
8. In 1992 includes local budget subsidies.
9. The definition of subsidies changed in 1991 to include only public institutions; subsidies and transfers to enterprises include subsidies to households, and subsidies and transfers to enterprises.
10. Central government housing fund included, value unknown in 1992.
11. 1992 subject to revision.
Sources: Ministry of the Economy and Finance and OECD calculations.

government has been successful in raising a number of excise taxes, and does not pay interest on its own debt, though this is for now a small item. Second, government expenditures have been supplemented with funds which are included in neither the budget nor extra-budgetary funds. Expenditures from the foreign asset and inventory revaluation account are off-budget (discussed below), and are basically inflation taxes whose expenditures are themselves inflationary. As discussed in Chapter III, many subsidies have come from monetary and credit policy, through debt write-offs and the extension of credit to agriculture and energy sectors at subsidised interest rates. But the principal explanation for the low budget deficits resides in the relationship of the state budget to state enterprises: enterprise taxation has increased with inflation, offsetting the effects of declining output.

The government was initially successful in substantially reducing government size in 1990 and 1991, but this progress was largely eroded in 1992: the general government share of expenditures fell from around 43 per cent in 1989 to near 36 per cent in 1991, but recovered to 40 per cent in 1992. The actual erosion has been even greater than these figures suggest because of the growing importance of off-budgetary funds. At the time of writing, the 1993 proposed budget foresees a decrease to 38 per cent.

Fiscal revenues

Under the old regime, with state enterprises an integral part of the state budget, profit remittances and taxes on net production were an important source of state revenues, accounting for around 40 per cent of general government revenue (Table 11). Firms were also responsible for paying social security, pension and wage taxes through payroll deductions, so that fiscal revenues received from firms accounted for 80 per cent of government revenues, essentially all except turnover taxes. In return, the budget was used as a method to reallocate these revenues for purposes of enterprise investments: capital expenditure accounted for about 40 per cent of total budget expenditures.

Despite tax and enterprise reforms, the dependency of the budget on the financial condition of state enterprises has stayed relatively constant. Along with a number of other tax reforms,[92] profit remittances and production taxes have been replaced with a profit tax which accounts for about 15 per cent of general government revenues; however, including taxes on the wage bill,[93] firms are still providing about 70 per cent of total revenues.[94] Additionally, firms were taxed at a rate of 50 per cent when inventories were revalued, as they were in late 1991. In 1992 new taxes were introduced on dividends (10 per cent), and sale of assets (20 per cent).

It is surprising that firms have been able to maintain profitability, and continue to provide profit tax revenues at all, given the dramatic declines in industrial production. The explanation for this conundrum lies in the distortions of the existing Romanian accounting system,[95] and its interaction with the triple-digit inflation which has prevailed over the last three years (these points are covered in more detail in Annex I). There are three principal areas where the effects are significant. The more important accounting distortion is that inventories are valued at historical cost, First-In-First-Out (FIFO) instead of Last-In-First-Out (LIFO). This type of accounting results in huge paper profits in a period of high inflation, upon which taxes are paid (the average and marginal rates of profit tax have converged at 45 per cent thanks to inflation). The combination of FIFO and profit taxes leaves firms with insufficient liquidity to replace inventory at current prices, generating negative cash flow.

The second distortion is inappropriate depreciation expenses, underestimating the economic costs. Fixed assets are carried on the basis of historical cost and have been revalued only once,[96] in April 1990 (during the conversion from state enterprises to commercial companies and *régies autonomes*), despite over 1 000 per cent inflation since that time. Undervaluation of fixed assets is compounded by straight-line depreciation methods and inappropriately long asset lives, in some cases as long as 100 years.

The third distortion is the treatment of costs. Costs, while recorded on an accrual basis, are only charged against income in proportion to the percentage of the value of production sold and cashed. Increases in stocks of raw materials, semi-finished and finished products are not charged until sold, and the latter are infrequently, if ever, written off.[97] Since most Romanian firms, especially state enterprises, set prices on a strict mark-up basis, they almost always show an operating profit (on mismeasured costs) no matter how little of final product they actually sell.

Estimates of the magnitude of these effects are necessarily crude, but do point to substantial sums. Use of realistic asset lives for depreciation would cut profits and profit taxes in half. Combined with any significant adjustment of fixed asset values, profits would be eliminated entirely, a prospect which appears likely when a new accounting system appropriately defining profit is introduced in 1994.

The most significant distortion would appear to lie in the FIFO treatment of inventories. Rough estimates (see Annex I) point to an overstatement of cash flow from this bias of around 1 700 billion lei in both 1991 and 1992: about 62 and 23 per cent of industrial production, respectively.[98]

The consequence of these distortions is that the budget is being balanced at the cost of decapitalising the enterprise sector. State firms have continued to pay substantial profit taxes when many, if not most, are in fact losing money if profits are correctly defined as the change in real net wealth. In consequence, these enterprises are under enormous cash-flow pressures. Firms appear to be meeting these demands by drastic cuts in investment spending, by only using cash to pay wages, and by creating arrears in inter-enterprise payments.

In contrast to industry, agriculture has benefited greatly from fiscal policy. Under the old regime, agricultural co-operatives contributed less than 1 per cent of total taxes, but relative prices were set so that enormous resources were transferred from agriculture to industry. As part of the land law, agricultural land which was privatised has been exempted from taxation for three years and profit taxes for five years. Most private produce is sold through private markets and is not subject to turnover tax, and the lack of an incomes tax means most farmers pay no taxes at all. Much of the rapidly expanding private sector, particularly in trade and services, also remains outside the reach of fiscal resources.

New sources of tax revenue appear unlikely, while old sources will come under increasing pressure. After some delays, a VAT is to be put in place in July 1993, but assuming this is introduced at rates comparable to other countries, it will yield revenues equivalent to the existing turnover tax, which it will replace. Plans exist to extend the current wage tax to become an income tax in 1994, and the exemption on agricultural profit taxes will expire that year. If the Romanian authorities are successful in lowering inflation substantially in 1993, profit tax revenues are likely to fall dramatically (even without changes in accounting methods). Similarly, it appears that labour shedding is finally beginning to reach proportions found in other CEECs – 1993 unemployment is projected at 13.5 per cent – so that the surpluses in extra-budgetary funds, and particularly the unemployment fund, are unlikely to be as large in 1993.[99]

Government expenditures

Expenditures from the general budget in 1991 and 1992 have been difficult to measure precisely because in both years there have been four budgets, and at the same time an increased resort to extra- and off-budgetary funds. There are two large off-budget funds which are not aggregated into the general government accounting: the revaluation of foreign assets fund, and counterpart funds from external official lending. There is also a small off-budget inventory (stock) revaluation fund.

Expenditures declined in both 1990 and 1991 by 3 per cent of GDP, as the government was successful in achieving its goal of reducing the influence of the budget in resource allocation. This trend was reversed in 1992 as the share of expenditures in GDP rebounded to 1990 levels. Underlying all of these movements was a marked shift in the composition of expenditures from investment in favour of consumption. State investment expenditures fell steadily from 40 per cent of the budget in 1989 to 20 per cent in 1990, and continued to decline to under 7 per cent in 1992: about 3 per cent of GDP. These have been replaced with subsidies and transfer payments. The 1993 budget anticipates a reversal of this trend with a complete elimination of consumer subsidies in May – an anticipated saving of 1 000 billion lei – and an increase in investment.

A great deal of the decline in investment spending was, to date, a result of the cancellation or mothballing of large, uneconomic prestige projects. Unfinished investment projects accounted for 1 500 billion lei in 1991 prices, about 75 per cent of GDP. However, the creation of commercial companies meant that the state also gave up responsibility for most investment spending in the economy. State investment remains in the budget only for the strategic sectors occupied by the *régies autonomes*, and in social and cultural areas, divided approximately equally between the two. Of state industrial investment, most is being allocated to the Cernovoda nuclear power plant, matching bilateral assistance from the Canadian government. Investment and maintenance in health, education and other social infrastructure is largely being deferred.

The government has been successful in containing the growth of wages and salaries; in fact government salaries are no longer competitive, causing a loss of skilled personnel to the growing private service sector. The growth in the share of current expenditures has been driven by the explosion of subsidies in 1991 and 1992, which now account for over 50 per cent of the state budget. The composition of subsidies has shifted away from covering enterprise losses towards subsidised consumer goods and agricultural inputs (Table 12); the production subsidies which remain are devoted almost entirely to the politically-sensitive mining sector. The government's desire to aid agriculture doubled its share in the 1992 budget and accounts for most of the increase in spending on economic actions (Table 11). The largest individual items are now subsidies on electrical energy and natural gas for the population, followed by meat, flour and fertilisers: these together account for 50 per cent of all subsidies.

The explosion of subsidies has occurred despite two rounds of subsidy cuts in May and September 1992. This apparent contradiction arises from several factors. Subsidies were raised substantially at the end of 1991, so that they did not affect the 1991 budget to any great extent. The cuts were calculated based on a percentage of the original nominal subsidy, while the actual subsidy was allowed to grow directly with inflation.[100] Since subsidies are heavily concentrated in areas where marginal costs are determined by imports and therefore by the exchange rate (*e.g.* electrical energy, fertilisers, bread), the large devaluations in November 1991 and over the summer of 1992 caused subsidies to increase sharply. As a result of this, the state budget deficit doubled from its predicted level of 2 per cent of GDP to 4 per cent of GDP in 1992. The sensitivity of budget outlays, particularly subsidies, to the exchange rate has led the Ministry of Finance, in early 1993, to call for the exchange rate to be stabilized at 500 lei/dollar (as incorporated in the projected budget in Table 11). At the time of writing, the budget is being revised at 600 lei/dollar, the current rate, making successful elimination of consumer subsidies in May imperative.

Extrabudgetary funds now comprise a growing portion of general government expenditures. Unemployment compensation was started in February 1991, and covers both dismissed workers and new entrants to the labour market, such as students completing diplomas. The unemployment and social security funds[101] together now account for around a quarter of general government spending, slightly less than equal to expenditures on subsidies. In both 1991 and 1992, budgeting for unemployment expenditures was

Table 12. **State budget subsidies**

Billion current lei

	1991	First budget 1992	Final budget 1992
Subsidies	151.6	375.7	508.2
To public institutions	4.3	9.8	14.9
To régies autonomes and state-owned			
commercial companies, *of which:*	48.5	75.3	104.3
Ministry of Industry	38.5	62.5	90.5
Ministry of Transportation	9.9	12.5	13.4
Ministry of Agriculture and			
Sylviculture	..	0.3	0.4
To cover cost/price differentials	98.9	290.6	389.0
Ministry of Industry	39.5	114.0	183.2
Electrical energy for the			
population			85.9
Chemicals and fertilisers			37.2
Natural gas for the population			21.7
Combustible energy for the			
population			16.3
Ministry of Agriculture and			
Sylviculture	46.3	156.8	181.6
Meat			62.8
Flour			47.3
Imported wheat			11.1
Edible oils			11.0
Ministry of Commerce and Tourism			12.7
Ministry of Transportation	8.2	14.3	16.4

Source: Ministry of Finance.

based on unemployment forecasts which proved to be too high.[102] The slower-than-expected pace of labour shedding meant that the unemployment fund accumulated surpluses in both years. Along with a comparable surplus on the social security account, these have been used to finance the unexpectedly high state budget deficit, allowing the general government budget to remain in balance.

Additional expenditures have been financed through off-budgetary accounts, which if added to the general government budget would increase expenditures by 15 per cent, or by 6 per cent of GDP. The most important of these is the foreign assets revaluation fund.[103] This fund derives from the effects of the exchange rate depreciation on the government's holdings of precious metals and foreign currency on deposit with the NBR.[104] In 1991 this account already exceeded the size of the unemployment fund, and in 1992 revenues were 198 billion lei, or 4 per cent of GDP. A total of about 95 billion lei from this account (73 billion lei in 1992) was used to recapitalise the four major banks in Romania, improving their balance sheets and accounting for the minimal use of the refinancing window during 1992. An even larger amount, to date over 120 billion lei, has been used to cover the impact of exchange rate changes on import payments by state enterprises.[105] (See Chapter III for a description of the price-fixing exchange rate.)

Table 13. **Extra- and off-budgetary funds of the state**

Billion lei

1991

	Extra-budgetary						Off-budget funds				
	Research	Health	Education	Unemploy-ment	Supplemen-tary pension	Social security	Stocks revaluation[1]	Sale of housing	Gold revaluation	Export promotion	Local govt. share of housing sales
Total expenditures	8.9	9.1		6.9	6.7	159.4	37.0	39.2	24.2	8.1	29.7
Total revenue	8.9	9.1		35.4	22.0	164.1	43.3	59.7	57.6	8.1	31.0
Overall balance	0.0	0.0		28.4	15.3	4.7	6.3	20.5	33.4	0.0	1.3

1992 – first version

	Extra-budgetary						Off-budget funds[2,3]			
	Research	Health	Education	Unemploy-ment	Supplemen-tary pension	Social security	Stocks revaluation[1]	Gold revaluation	Restructuring[4]	Foreign loans[5]
Beginning balance							8.9	33.4	7.7	76.0
Total expenditures	36.0	40.9	8.6	108.2	23.0	407.6	36.1	207.0	11.8	300.0
Total revenue	36.0	38.9	8.6	83.6	50.5	415.3	28.5	198.2	9.1	224.0
Overall balance	0.0	-2.0	0.0	-24.6	27.5	7.7	1.3	24.6	5.0	

1992 – realised

	Extra-budgetary						Off-budget funds[2]			
	Research	Health	Education	Unemploy-ment	Supplemen-tary pension	Social security	Stocks revaluation[1]	Gold revaluation	Restructuring[4]	Foreign loans[5]
Beginning balance							8.9	33.4	7.7	76.0
Total expenditures	42.7	36.4	6.7	44.9	25.4	406.6	36.1	207.0	11.8	300.0
Total revenue	43.8	34.3	8.7	136.8	74.5	468.8	28.5	198.2	9.1	224.0
Overall balance	1.1	-2.1	2.0	91.9	49.1	62.2	1.3	24.6	5.0	

1. Financed through 50% of the adjustment in value due to revaluation.
2. Off-budget funds are not included in the general or consolidated budgets.
3. Assumed to be the same as realised 1992.
4. In 1991 this was the fund from sales of housing.
5. Counterpart to domestic currency.
Source: Ministry of Finance.

Another 14 billion lei were used to supplement subsidies to the mining sector, with additional small amounts helping cover subsidies on various food items.

The other major off-budget account is the counterpart fund from foreign currency loans to the government by official lenders.[106] The inflow into this fund amounted to 140 billion lei in 1992. This sum, which is low in comparison to the foreign currency actually disbursed, apparently arises either from delays in payments by importers resulting from arrears (especially true of energy imports) or from conversion of funds into lei at the artificial exchange rate of 180 lei/dollar. The government plans to use these funds as a source of investment capital. To date about 75 billion lei have been invested, including, 46 billion lei in recapitalising the meat processing industry, 25 billion lei in recapitalising clearing accounts for trade with socialist and former socialist countries, and 15 billion lei in the Bucharest-Constanza highway project.

Local government

The government is currently in the process of devolving responsibilities onto local governments. These are composed of county councils and local municipal councils with mayors. Currently, they are responsible for maintenance of roads and local transport services. A process of transferring parts of the state patrimony to local governments began in the summer of 1992. It is being bogged down in the debate over the division of responsibilities for providing government services between state and local government. Local governments want to gain physical assets which maximise income, while avoiding responsibility for provision of costly services.

Currently local government is accounting for nearly 10 per cent of general government expenditures. These are being financed with transfers from the state budget (81 per cent in 1992) supplemented by its 50 per cent share of earnings from housing privatisation. A law is now pending before Parliament to permit local governments to levy taxes, including land and real property taxes. Local governments will also be able to borrow money, but this must be approved by referendum.

Budget financing

To date, state budget deficits have been entirely financed by the central bank, or offset with the deposits of off- and extra-budgetary funds, which are on deposit with the commercial banks. In the future these funds are likely to have smaller surpluses, while financing by monetary creation will not be possible: it is limited by the Romanian Constitution to five times the capital and reserves of the National Bank, which currently stands at 2.5 billion lei. Financing of the 1993 state government deficit, even if constant in real terms at around 250 billion lei, will therefore require innovative methods.

In December 1992, the Government made available a trial issue of 3.3 billion lei in government bonds to the public, the first of four issues contemplated this year.[107] As of early January 1993, total sales have been around 300 million lei, and are occurring at a daily rate of 20 million lei. The government anticipates being able to raise 100 billion lei through this method over the course of the year.[108] Additionally, the government is considering not transferring the Savings Bank to the State Ownership Fund, as had been originally planned (see Annex III). Instead, by maintaining direct control over the Savings Bank, the Romanian authorities would be able to finance the remaining government deficit directly with Savings Bank deposits.[109]

Assessment

At first glance, fiscal policy appears to have been a success story for Romania. Fiscal balance has been maintained in the face of declining output, increased needs for social protection, and the administrative confusion which can often accompany tax reform. Budget deficits since the Revolution have been much smaller than those occurring in other CEECs.

Nonetheless there are grounds for concern. On the revenue side, the budget has been balanced at the cost of decapitalising state enterprises, fuelling the creation of enterprise arrears, and inhibiting supply response in the economy. Firms, by hoarding labour, have eased budgetary pressures by creating surpluses in the unemployment and social security funds, but again at the cost of adjustment. The introduction of Western accounting procedures, originally planned for 1993, has been postponed until 1994. When introduced, these procedures could dramatically reduce profit taxes unless there is a turn-around in real enterprise profitability. At the same time, growth sectors such as peasant agriculture have been deliberately exempted from any fiscal burden.

On the expenditure side, the budget does not accurately reflect the use of foreign asset revaluation accounts, debt forgiveness programs, interest rate subsidies by the NBR, and losses of state enterprises financed by inter-enterprise arrears. The true size of the deficit has probably been well over 5 per cent of GDP rather than the near budget balance actually recorded.

Romanian fiscal policy has been conducted with a short-term horizon, reactively and *ad hoc*, sacrificing long-term structural changes to deal with immediate pressures. The prime example of this is the expenditure of enormous funds on subsidies and particularly those to support the use of an unrealistic accounting exchange rate for particular industries. The direct result of this has been that the Ministry of Finance has opposed a more realistic exchange rate policy. Resources wasted on subsidies could be redirected towards needs-tested social programs and much-needed investment in social infrastructure and restructuring of industry. Of equal import, these types of expenditures have slowed the government's role in direct microeconomic intervention in the economy through elimination of price controls and central allocation and caused a rebound in the relative size of government expenditures in the economy. They create a serious danger that a pattern of expenditures driven by rent-seeking and regulatory capture could become permanently established in Romania.

Wage policy

In line with other CEECs, wage controls have been an important element of the stabilization programme. Until April 1991, wages were centrally established by branch according to laws covering salary structure. In the drive for greater freedom marking the post-Revolution period, negotiation of salaries and wages was introduced: Law 14 permitted salaries and wages to be freely negotiated. The danger of a wage explosion was recognised in the design of the stabilization programme leading the authorities to consider two schemes for tax-based wage control: control of individual wages or control of the total wage bill. The former was adopted in 1991 since it was considered that the total wage bill was likely to have been highly distorted by central planning. The disadvantage of the chosen base became apparent during 1991. It was evident that enterprises were not being forced to economise on employment while at the same time it was not possible to rationalise the wage structure. Overall, the incomes policy introduced in January 1991 was difficult to monitor and obstructed the development of labour markets. To encourage flexibility in the wage structure, the base for tax-based controls for 1992 was switched to the total wage bill. The new system applies to all commercial companies with majority state ownership and to *régies autonomes*. These enterprises may set individual wages and salaries at any level above the minimum wage, but increases in the total wage bill above a given limit are taxed prohibitively.

At the centre of the policy is the principle of partial indexation to expected inflation. However, the policy allows for *ex-post*corrections of the indexation coefficient when actual inflation differs substantially from that expected. Indexation represented limits on maximum wage growth in 1991 or the total wage bill in 1992; whether it was in fact granted depended on lower-level bargaining between unions and enterprises. The coefficient of indexation had to be approved by the government, taking into account the trade unions' opinion. The institutional structure for this dialogue was substantially improved in December 1991 when the National Commission for Indexation was established, charged with achieving a consensus on incomes policy.

Following the two big price adjustments in November 1990 and April 1991, wage increases were agreed to ensure a 60 per cent compensation for the average consumer budget. To this end, in April 1991 a supplement of 2 500 lei was granted to all workers. This resulted in a substantial recovery of the real wage but also compressed an already narrow salary structure still further (from 1:4 to 1:3, whereas 1:6 is regarded by the authorities as more ''normal''). For the period April to December, a 40 per cent indexation coefficient was adopted. The price surge in November 1991 forced revisions: the indexation coefficient was established at 50 per cent, and an *ex-post* correction of the coefficient was agreed with unions in order to maintain the average real wage at 80 per cent of the October 1991 level.

For 1992, the 50 per cent indexation to expected inflation was supplemented by a 100 per cent compensation for reduction in consumer subsidies: in May and September, flat wage increases fully compensated for the reduction of consumer subsidies.[110]This brought the government closer to meeting its commitment of maintaining wages (rather than the wage bill) at 80 per cent of October 1991 levels. In November the average coefficient was established at 65.5 per cent.

Attempts have been made to minimise the microeconomic distortions associated with most wage controls. In order to ameliorate the potential anti-employment bias of the scheme, higher wage norms are available to expanding firms: the costs of increased employment are deducted 100 per cent from the norm for ''productive activity'', 60 per cent otherwise. There have also been experiments in 1992 to adjust the wage base according to the change in the ratio of profits to wages between 1992 and 1991. However, the adjustment has not been greatly used as for most firms the ratio is under unity.

Although a reduction in real wages has occurred, wage policy has up till now been used primarily as an anti-inflation instrument. However, in the light of changing terms of trade, including new energy prices, and the need to restructure, a more flexible real wage policy may be necessary. Such a development might be encouraged if the accounting system gave a more accurate impression of the parlous state of enterprises: profits simply do not exist to protect both real wages and employment.

V.   Conclusions

In spite of widespread perceptions to the contrary, Romania has in fact undertaken major reforms over the past three years. The legal framework for a market economy is largely in place, although effective implementation is still lagging. Reforms to the fiscal and financial systems have been enacted and new policy instruments have been developed. A corporate profits tax has been implemented and a start has been made on decentralising government to lower, autonomous levels. Agricultural co-operatives have been dismantled and private ownership of agricultural land re-established. More importantly, the voluntary nature of economic organisation and initiative is slowly being created in agriculture. In industry, the framework of an ambitious mass privatisation programme is largely in place. Starting from practically a zero base, the private sector is once more emerging: progress has been particularly marked in the privatisation of the retail system where the private sector now accounts for around 45 per cent of sales. Foreign trade has been substantially liberalised and the share of the private sector in this activity has expanded quickly to around 25 per cent of both exports and imports. After falling in 1990 and 1991, exports have finally begun to expand in the course of 1992, rising by some 14 per cent. Foreign direct investment, once reviled, is now actively supported and is growing, particularly in the energy exploration sector.

Starting from extremely difficult initial conditions there has also been progress in the macroeconomic area. A stabilization programme has been pursued since 1991 and will be continued. Targets for credit and money growth have generally been reached and the monetary overhang probably eliminated. Growth of nominal wages has been contained. The share of budgetary incomes, and to a much lesser extent expenditures, in GDP has been reduced while at the same time the state budget deficit has been limited to about 2-3 per cent of GDP.

Notwithstanding these achievements, the situation remains critical, with the foundations for a sustained recovery and transformation not yet laid. Production has continued to fall, with few indications of the levelling-out noted in other countries. Inflation remains high and volatile. International reserves are low, covering only a few weeks' imports, while the market exchange rate has continued to fall. Control over the budget risks becoming increasingly difficult: inflation-related taxes on enterprises remain vital for budget revenue, but are serving to decapitalise them, and social expenditures are continuing to grow.

While in the circumstances facing Romania a policy of gradual reform was perhaps inevitable, the way in which gradualism has been pursued by the Romanian authorities has been costly. Gradual reforms have been pursued by many countries, notably those in Asia, but in the successful cases the overriding political objective was to achieve growth and structural transformation; interest groups which would hold back the process were by-passed. By contrast, gradualism in Romania has meant in practice support for the existing enterprises and mix of output. The influence of interest groups which serve to block reforms has been strong: the challenge is to develop a consensus within the society to sustain reform.

Both structural reform objectives and stabilization goals have been undermined by the fact that at times the microeconomic or financial policy measures have been diluted by bureaucratic interventions in the face of market responses unacceptable to them. Gradualism always carried with it the danger of pathological market outcomes until complementary reforms were enacted. Rather than accepting these as unavoidable transition costs and accelerating the reform process, the reverse has occurred in some important cases: the malfunctioning of markets has been taken as a signal for increased administrative action rather than as a sign for faster implementation of reform. This has been especially true of price reforms and agricultural policy, where interest groups have been particularly active in defending their positions. While policy may have succeeded in mitigating declines in employment, ensuring basic consumer needs and attenuating income losses in the very short term, the costs have been high. The overall effect of gradualism in Romania has been to prolong the duration of the output decline as elements of the shortage economy have persisted, leaving inflation high and the currency effectively inconvertible.

The priority given to protecting living standards has not in fact succeeded in limiting the fall in aggregate output, but has undermined the ability of the authorities to pursue consistent reform policies. In Romania, the fundamental cause for the output drop is often viewed as being shortages of inputs, above all energy and raw materials imports, leading to idle capacity. This is a misperception: the output decline, now in its fifth year, is essentially a structural phenomenon reflecting primarily the lack of adjustment to balance of payments conditions and new world prices. Indeed, large amounts of the available energy and raw-material inputs have been absorbed in the production of inventories that cannot be sold, and to this extent a focus on aggregate output measures is misplaced. Misperception of the nature of the problem has contributed to policy inconsistency: when economic policy has been faced with the dilemma of either supporting unproductive activities at a cost of sacrificing monetary, fiscal or structural reform goals, or imposing financial discipline (including economic prices) and facing higher unemployment and firm closures, the former option has been taken more often than not.

Excessive swings in money and credit growth and frequent special measures to bail out financially distressed sectors have undermined credibility in monetary policy despite intentions to pursue tight policy, and this has been reflected in the foreign exchange market. Excess asset demand for foreign exchange presently exists at almost any exchange rate since domestic currency is not seen as a credible store of value. From the real economy, demand for foreign exchange is largely price-inelastic as firms with soft budget constraints (increasingly in the form of preferential credits) continue to receive import allocations. Under these circumstances, devaluations have become part of a vicious circle with inflation expectations – while the needed reallocation of resources toward traded goods is minimised. Romania lacks a nominal anchor, so that inflation remains high and unstable, exacting a real price on the economy.

In sum, a fundamental change in the implementation of the reform strategy is now necessary if the reform momentum is to be maintained and its fruits eventually realised. The government programme, approved by Parliament in March 1993, goes some way in this direction but a great deal will depend on whether it can be effectively implemented. In moving ahead, the key will be to establish clear priorities, and to ensure that actions taken across the board are consistent with these. Two immediate systemic objectives would seem to deserve top priority: adapting to a constrained balance-of-payments situation, and consolidating the development of a monetary economy by making the lei a fully credible store of value. To achieve these, action is needed above all in three interrelated areas: the financial discipline of enterprises has to be strengthened, prices have to be allowed to play their proper role in clearing markets, and the currency has to be made fully convertible for current transactions and the exchange rate stabilized. These three elements are tightly interdependent and need to be seen together. Actions on only one or two fronts, if not supported by action on the third, would fail. Conversely, if rapid progress can be made in these three areas, the constraints imposed by the balance of payments would ease relatively quickly, and financial disorder would dissipate, easing the task of moving ahead with further reforms.

The imposition of financial discipline on enterprises is fundamental. This has proven difficult in all CEECs and it is probably inevitable that tightening will be gradual. What is important, however, is that the direction be maintained. Over the past two years, many promises of action in this area have not been implemented, leading to a decline in policy credibility. This has been reinforced by a drawn-out programme of enterprise debt forgiveness. In tightening financial discipline, several measures should be considered as a priority:

- The small number of loss-making firms including those with negative cash flows (said to be around 110), which have been identified as making a major contribution to inter-enterprise arrears, should be closed. Pending their closure, losses should be absorbed by the budget in order to make clearer the true financial position of the government. While the pursuit of a low budget deficit is important (thereby avoiding government dis-saving at a time of shortage of savings) there is no point in doing this by price controls or accounting tricks, whereby budget responsibilities are directed either to the banking system or to off-budget accounts. Credit injections for the settlement of inter-enterprise arrears, selective or not, need to be avoided in present circumstances, as they are serving to promote expectations that firms in financial difficulty will be saved by government action. Firms should be required to pay interest on their debts to other enterprises at a rate at least as high as for bank borrowing.
- An important element in tightening financial discipline will be an effective implementation of the bankruptcy law already in existence and the urgent development of a new one more appropriate for the institutional capacities of Romania. With the assumption of ownership of the commercial companies by the State Ownership Fund (SOF) and the five Private Ownership Funds (POFs), it will be vital that these Funds do not undercut the spirit of the legislation: they need to enforce financial discipline at the level of the individual enterprises and to end the "solidarity" between firms whereby actions prejudicial to another are avoided. There is a danger that, in the name of restructuring, firms will not follow financial discipline, but will expect assistance from the SOF in particular.
- Foreign exchange deposits of enterprises should not remain protected from creditors. Any change in this regulation will have to be closely co-ordinated with reforms to bankruptcy procedures to avoid enterprises and the public viewing this regulatory change as a form of expropriation of coveted foreign exchange. In

addition, the use of foreign exchange deposits as collateral for lei advances from the banks should be terminated or, better still, interest rates increased to make the practice unprofitable. Both practices have been encouraged so as to strengthen incentives for enterprises to export, and so to support the exchange rate, but as they encourage financial indiscipline, are counterproductive.

In moving out of the policy impasse, it will be necessary to reduce uncertainty and to eliminate distortions to resource allocation by removing rapidly the remaining price controls – including the widespread controls on profit margins. The need for investment is stressed by all in Romania, but price and profit controls have functioned as a disincentive: the expected rate of profit has been depressed, and realised profits have been insufficient to finance required investments. Preferential credits at low interest rates are no substitute. Speed in liberalising prices is now essential because, given the experience of the last three years, a drawn-out price reform is unlikely to be credible. Full price liberalisation, however, requires complementary measures:

- The Romanian economy is dominated by monopolies and tight oligopolies, which leads to fears that full price liberalisation would produce an irrational price structure and inflation. While it is hard to believe that even monopolies could produce a price structure with so much uncertainty and irrationality as at present, the lack of competition is indeed an important issue. A rapid move to convertibility would stimulate competition but a more active approach to competition policy is certainly also necessary. The fate of new legislation currently before the Parliament remains unclear but there is a danger that it could place unwarranted stress on price controls and price surveillance as instruments for controlling monopoly power, and too little emphasis on the need to create an independent competition authority. However, in the Romanian context a greater responsibility lies with the owners: the SOF and POFs. They need to encourage competition among their companies even if, as a result of smaller monopoly rents, privatisation proceeds are reduced. To help resolve these issues, the competition office might be empowered to make published interventions before the Funds. Perhaps such advice should be made more persuasive by empowering the competition office to directly dismantle state-created, privately-owned firms enjoying dominant positions. With a top-down approach to restructuring there is also a danger that the promotion of competition will be seen as a superfluous luxury rather than as an integral part of the continuing restructuring process.
- To be effective, price liberalisation has to be accompanied by the removal of the remaining mechanisms by which a few essential goods are still administratively allocated, both in agriculture and industry. This will be difficult to do, for important elements of the bureaucracy are accustomed to dealing with "shortages" by regulatory instruments, often arguing that the lack of market mechanisms prevents any alternative. The development of market responses has thus been inhibited and distorted. This vicious circle needs to be finally overcome. There will of course be activities for which the government may wish to ensure a particular resource flow. In such cases this should be done solely through economic instruments such as taxes or subsidies.

The exchange rate regime has been one of the most unsatisfactory elements of the transformation programme to date, with damaging micro- and macroeconomic consequences. Urgent steps are necessary in which the exchange rate will no longer be treated as if it were an instrument of policy, but as an intermediate objective requiring appropriate instruments for its support. These steps are necessary with or without a stabilization fund, although implementation may increase the likelihood that such a fund would find international support. The objective of exchange rate policy should not just be stability but also convertibility. Several steps are necessary:

- Rapid price liberalisation and improved financial discipline are necessary instruments for the stabilization of the exchange rate: they introduce market mechanisms into the allocation of scarce foreign exchange, improving the responsiveness of supply and demand to exchange rate changes. At the same time, the remaining quantitative allocation of foreign exchange needs to be terminated.
- A more active interest rate policy will be necessary, at least in the short run, to overcome the deep-seated inflation expectations. Rapid price liberalisation could lead to a short-term surge in inflation, and therefore entail high nominal interest rates for a time. But thereafter expectations would be subject to less uncertainty, allowing interest rates to decline as the lei gained credibility as a store of value and a reliable unit of account. The increase in nominal interest rates during 1992 was strongly criticised in Romania so that a more active policy will be controversial. However, higher nominal rates in 1992 were not associated with the complementary policy measures that would have been needed to establish credibility, and were undermined by increased arrears. Moreover, price controls led to distorted signals: controls on producer prices led to high *ex-post* real rates of interest for producers, but higher consumer price inflation led to negative rates for savers for the year as a whole.

Restructuring of the economy is a major priority for the government, which appears to be taking a top-down approach to the process. At first the SOF was given implicit authority to undertake restructuring; but more recently there have been suggestions that this should remain the responsibility of the state, the argument being that the SOF lacks appropriate manpower. This is a worrying development which would hold back the development of market relations and may be difficult to reconcile with improved financial discipline. But the view that the SOF could indeed be responsible is also debatable. To establish a process of restructuring – in the broadest sense of the concept – a number of measures are necessary:

- Price and exchange rate reform, improved financial discipline and increased competition are necessary for restructuring. Shortcomings in these areas have acted as barriers to restructuring. Only then will it be possible to identify those activities that would be uncompetitive under almost any restructuring, and to identify new opportunities.
- The government has made the promotion of exports a major plank of its strategy and this is to be welcomed. However, rather than doing this by removing the major structural barriers identified above, it is proposing preferential credits, administrative allocation of inputs, and diverse tax incentives. These measures are generally undesirable and will only contribute to new attempts by interest groups to promote their own interests. They also do not assure that exports develop for those activities which are truly viable, and indeed may leave such activities unidentified.
- Restructuring should in the first instance remain the responsibility of the enterprises, with the owners (*i.e.* the Ownership Funds) checking only on expected

profitability and in particular the rate of return to investment. Detailed involvement on the part of the Funds and Ministries should be avoided, for this will open the process to influence by pressure groups and hold back the development of managerial responsibility.

- In the government programme, great stress has been laid on the development of management contracts for enterprises which will specify performance criteria and responsibilities. The Ownership Funds are also developing similar contracts for their staff and board representatives. In principle, management contracts are important, serving to clarify the current uncertain status of firms awaiting privatisation and perhaps even serving to improve their performance – though the evidence on this point in OECD countries is still unclear. However, to achieve these results management contracts must be carefully constructed, emphasising clear-cut goals and incentives. Preliminary indications are that this will not be the case in Romania: the criteria may include profitability, export orientation, "completing of internal consumption" and decreasing consumption of raw materials and energy. The danger is that goals are being set which are not compatible, introducing a new element of negotiation with the Ownership Funds. Under conditions of distorted prices, profit is often a misleading measure of performance as well, but the answer is not to replace it with administrative criteria. Rather it is to liberalise prices, which would simplify the difficult task of specifying appropriate contracts.

- Under present thinking, the banks appear to have very little role in the process of restructuring, being seemingly relegated to passive financial restructuring after the real enterprise restructuring has occurred. This would result in banks remaining underdeveloped, and promote the maintenance of a passive monetary economy. Banks should be assigned an active role, which will need to be supported by technical assistance in the training of bank staff, and by selective bank recapitalisation.

- Some highly capital-intensive industries may well require special treatment. In this case they should be isolated from the Ownership Funds, which will then be free to concentrate on privatisation and the monitoring of enterprise performance.

- As noted above, the break-up of firms to encourage competition and efficiency needs to be promoted. Claims by existing managements that synergies must be preserved should be treated with caution.

A vital part of the restructuring process is privatisation. After inevitable initial delay, Romania has nearly in place the institutions to support a mass privatisation programme, including the widespread distribution of vouchers. Although it has many attractive aspects, the nearer the plan comes to implementation the further it seems to diverge from its original intentions.

- In line with original proposals, the privatisation process should remain as decentralised as possible. In practice this means accelerating the development of the POFs and delegating to them considerable authority for privatising their enterprises. In addition, the relations of the Funds with each other and with the various Ministries urgently requires clarification. This is especially true with respect to pre-privatisation restructuring responsibilities. As mentioned earlier, the competition office should play an important role in that process. The degree of enterprise independence in the pre-privatisation phase also needs to be better defined along sound market-oriented lines.

- At least for small-scale firms, though possibly for medium ones also, the government's preferred choice of privatisation method appears to be favouring management and employee buyouts (MEBO): the insider option. Vouchers will be used to support the process as well as favourable credit facilities from the SOF. While this method may raise questions of equity, it has the strong advantage of allowing privatisation to be accomplished with speed. To reach the final objectives of privatisation – owners with an interest in preserving and increasing the value of their enterprises – it will be necessary to view the MEBO as possibly the start of the process and to allow further sales of shares by the new owners with few restrictions. Current proposals forbidding resale for a period, or limiting resale to other insiders, would limit this quite severely.
- There would appear to be substantial barriers to the development of new private enterprises such as access to premises and to machinery and equipment. Urgent attention needs to be given to removing these barriers and to avoiding the creation of new ones. In this respect, the restrictions on the resale of assets acquired during privatisation should be eliminated.

The above policy reforms, by re-establishing coherence and consistency, would make the path for monetary policy easier: the transmission mechanism from control of nominal aggregates to inflation would be more effective. Monetary policy should therefore remain on its generally tight path, with the stop-go policies evident at some times in the past to be avoided. However, given the large inherent uncertainties in defining appropriate rates of expansion for money or credit aggregates in an economy in transition, more weight will need to be given to the exchange rate in the conduct of monetary policy.

Fiscal policy will have to be increasingly oriented to planning for pressures which will arise as inflation-linked taxes start to decline and social expenditures to increase. Reforms are urgently required to the accounting system which would increase depreciation allowances for firms and lower taxes on inventory profits arising from inflation. This would have a major effect on revenues so that it is important that the VAT be introduced as planned in 1993 and that steps be continued leading to the introduction of a full income tax in 1994. Moreover, while in order to maintain its credibility the government must stick to its policy of no taxes on agricultural land and profits for the next three and five years respectively, it is important to make it quite clear that at the end of the period the exemption will be lifted.

The reform programme has overwhelmed the legislative and administrative capacities of the country, contributing to policy inconsistency. Policy initiatives have often been poorly co-ordinated across Ministries and alternatives not carefully investigated. Both in the Parliament and in the government, too little attention has been devoted to efficient implementation of policy, including the founding of new institutions. At the highest levels, the Council of Ministers is frequently overwhelmed with minutiae. The establishment of the Ministry of Economic Reform and Strategy with broad co-ordinating powers is therefore to be welcomed. However, high-level commitment will be needed over some time to ensure success, since the way individual Ministries function will also have to change – including the tendency to be secretive with one another. Particular attention will also have to be devoted to reforming the budget process, to assist in reallocating public revenues and controlling expenditures. Improving legislative and administrative capacities is not exclusively a matter of increased resources but of more efficient use of the considerable manpower already allocated. An accelerated withdrawal of administrative intervention as advocated here would ease the burdens, allowing more attention to be devoted to general policy issues.

Fundamentally, in order to achieve consistency in the reform effort, the authorities will have to alter their approach of seeking to protect the population from income loss through supporting the current levels and structure of production: some factories will have to close and, depending on the evolution of wages, there will be increased unemployment as firms reduce over-manning. What is urgently required is not an abandonment of social concerns, for the object of the transition to a market economy is not to make people worse off for the sake of it, but to redefine policy instruments and objectives in a consistent manner. The overall objective must be to free resources for investment and away from consumption while at the same time providing basic social protection: to give some idea of what is involved, out of 2.9 billion dollars of foreign loans contracted by the state, only 9 per cent have been used for development purposes, the remainder being devoted to consumption. Several points might stimulate this reassessment (which is already under way):

– The construction of a social safety net has followed lines established in OECD countries by having as its core an unemployment insurance programme. The surplus in this insurance fund has been used to support the budget: in effect, to finance consumption. This may not be the best way to proceed in an economy in transition rather than one experiencing cyclical downturns. Funds could perhaps be better used to support worker mobility, or the establishment of new ventures through, for example, capitalising unemployment benefits. Given the large adjustments that workers will have to make in adapting to a market economy, unemployment benefits might only be made available in conjunction with retraining programmes that promote such adjustment. Such programmes might range from developing new skills to simply keeping workers in contact with the labour force in firms which are no longer actively engaged in production.

– Particular attention will need to be paid to youth unemployment. State enterprises are adjusting work force levels slowly through natural attrition, which means that new jobs are not becoming available in existing firms; yet the development of new activities and private firms is still held back, so that unemployment risks becoming more and more concentrated on new entrants into the labour market.

– Savings must be made in social benefits and other social expenses through careful targeting of groups at risk, rather than through subsidies that at present provide benefits in a non-discriminating manner. The resources saved need to be made available for the development of the economy, as this alone holds out the prospect of sustained social support.

A specific feature of the Romanian economy is the large stock of unfinished investment projects inherited from the previous regime: sunk costs in these projects may amount to around 75 per cent of GNP. Regardless of the method of financing – from the budget or the banking system – such projects should only be completed after rigorous cost-benefit analysis has been completed which explicitly recognises the high opportunity cost of investment funds in Romania: the rate of return to investment is of primary importance. In many cases, under present distorted conditions such assessments are practically impossible. This suggests a very cautious approach to many of these projects until reforms are in a more advanced stage.

Starting from the most difficult conditions – the political, social and economic inheritance of the Ceausescu period, including a savage compression of consumption during the 1980s – Romania has in fact accomplished a great deal over the last three years. Although at the cost of severe macroeconomic destabilization, the grounds for a return to civil society were laid in 1990. In 1991 and 1992 considerable macroeconomic and structural reform was carried out. This was achieved in the face of severe external financial restrictions and lack of external support, which was either not forthcoming or was not available at critical moments when it would have served to buttress resolve in taking difficult decisions. As stressed in this report, changes are once again necessary in the reform programme so as to move the process forward in a coherent and consistent manner. This is the challenge for the Romanian authorities – one of which they are fully aware – and for the political process. The challenge for the OECD countries will be to lend support at the critical moments. Acting together can open the way for Romania to overcome its present difficulties and to establish the basis for a modern economy and society.

Notes and references

1. The litany of horror stories about life during the last years of the Ceausescu regime is tragic and depressing. Many relate to the lack of energy for the population: little or no heat, hot water or electricity in the face of severe winters. "The quality of life deteriorated during the 1980s to a startling extent. At the end of the decade, Romania ranked at or close to the bottom among the countries of Europe on virtually all indicators: health, housing conditions, clean air, access to radio and television, services, education, transportation, and so on. It was called the 'Ethiopia of Europe'." See Nestor Ratesh, *Romania: The Entangled Revolution,* Center for Strategic and International Studies, The Washington Papers, 152. Washington, DC: Praeger, 1991, p. 8.

2. Gross output decreased but inputs such as fertilizers and energy fell further, the net effect being an increase in value-added. Whether such a situation represented an increase in efficiency, and is therefore sustainable, is still unclear.

3. See J. Montias, "The Romanian economy: a survey of current problems", *European Economy,* No. 2, 1991.

4. Before 1990 the special average exchange rate for exports was lei 27-30 per dollar, while for imports it was lei 15-16. The difference was covered by the budget. In early 1990 the exchange rate was unified at 21 lei to the dollar which deterred production for exports. See *Monetary policy in the transition period,* National Bank of Romania, Bucharest, November 1992.

5. Conventionally defined, the budget was in surplus in 1990. However, when allowance is made for fiscal responsibilities which were shifted to the banking sector, such as enterprise losses, a substantial deficit of around 10 per cent emerges. See J. Montias, *op. cit.*

6. In line with historical practice there were many goods-specific exchange rates throughout the first nine months of 1990. For purposes of comparison, an average exchange rate, certainly overvalued, of 21 lei/dollar, is utilised. At the end of December 1992 the official exchange rate reached 460 lei/dollar.

7. The share of imports in GDP is small, which would appear to dampen the impact of the exchange rate on inflation. This is, however, misleading. Pressure on the exchange rate reflects lack of confidence in the currency and therefore a decline in money demand. This will directly influence inflation. Moreover, despite the small share of imports in GDP, tradeable goods prices will nevertheless be influenced, even if only administratively, by adjustments to world prices.

8. The surplus on tourist earnings generated under Ceausescu has been eliminated now that Romanians can travel abroad. The expatriate Romanian community is relatively small, limiting unrequited transfers and labour remittances.

9. New commitments by the EC for 1992 amounted to 180 million dollars.

10. This partly reflected the fall in domestic investment: the largest fall was in imports of machinery and equipment in hard currency. Imports of machinery and equipment in non-convertible currencies actually rose.

11. The corresponding profit ratio for the private sector declined from 16 per cent to around 12 per cent. The private sector is, however, highly concentrated in particular industries. Mimeo, Ministry of Reform, Bucharest, 1993.

12. Montias, *op cit.*

13. Both Kuwait and Iraq were important markets for Romania before the Gulf War. In addition, Iraq owed about 1.7 billion dollars. Before the invasion of Kuwait it had been arranged that the debt would be repaid in oil deliveries but this was frozen at the time the international embargo came into force. The repayment of another debt, also in oil, owed by Iran was delayed until late 1992. Romania has also been adversely affected by the embargo on Yugoslavia.

14. For Hungary the ratio is around unity. See International Energy Agency, Paris, *Energy Survey of Poland,* and *Energy Survey of Hungary.*

15. These include a sharp reduction in the work week and the removal of compulsion in a great deal of economic activity.

16. BBC *Summary of World Broadcasts,* No. 1368, 30 April 1992.

17. Of the remainder, 16 per cent goes to households. This is exceptionally small by international standards although it did increase from an even lower level following the ending of restrictions in 1990.

18. It was prepared by a twenty-member commission made up of mostly administration officials, in consultation with over 2 000 Romanian academics, enterprise managers, trade unionists, scientists and civil servants.

19. The second phase was to focus on modernisation of the economy over a five-year period.

20. "... the production of goods indispensable for the population ... will be co-ordinated through the targets of the Plan of the national economy. The plan of the economy will comprise compulsory (firm) targets attainable in form of state orders. These orders ensure the production ... [to] ensure the stock of goods for the population's supply, defence, social security."

"State orders will also supply the economic agents with the raw materials and electricity as well as other scarce products coming from domestic production or import", see Council for Reform, *The White Book of the Romanian Reform,* Bucharest, 1991.

21. Enterprise targets were expected to be 40-50 per cent of economic activity in 1991, falling to 20-30 per cent in 1992, and were to supplemented with indirect methods of economic control: budget and bank credits, and tax incentives. Council for Reform, *op. cit.,* p. 9.

22. For a more detailed review see C. Grey, P. Ianachkov. R. Hanson., *Romania's evolving legal framework for private sector development,* World Bank, WPS 872, 1992.

23. Under the old regime permission had to be obtained to move between towns. Officially, all large cities were closed to new immigrants.

24. C. Gray, R. Hanson and P. Ianachkov, *op. cit.*

25. There are many grounds for this. The monopsonistic and monopolistic nature of Romanian industry means that commitments may be altered unilaterally. However, there also appears to be an extraordinary "solidarity" between firms (*e.g.* money is said to be lent between firms for the payment of wages) which might be a product of a belief that, at the end of the day, none will be let go by the government.

26. This is often confused in popular debate with short-termism. In fact "profit maximisation" in this instance refers to the maximisation of net present value (*i.e.* wealth) by the owner.

27. Initially there were around 200. Possible explanations for the increase are the creation of new RAs by local governments to provide services, and the division into separate regional companies of national RAs as part of the government's drive for decentralisation.

28. The current owner is the relevant ministry. For CCs, during the course of 1993 the owner will become the Ownership Funds. See Annex III.

29. For further discussion of this concept in the context of CEECs, see E. Hinds, *Issues in the Introduction of Market Forces in Eastern European Socialist Economies,* World Bank, 1990, and the Economic Survey of Poland, OECD, 1992.

30. The new government elected in October 1992 has affirmed its intention to reimpose some accountability on state firms through the use of management performance contracts, which are to be introduced beginning in February 1993. See Annex III for further details.

31. J. M. Montias, *op. cit.*

32. As quoted in Montias, *op. cit.*

33. Leasing of assets to private entrepreneurs was made possible by Law 15/1990, which reorganised the state-owned enterprises. The methods which could be used were detailed in Government Decision 1228.

34. This was by Law 31, which also had the effect of nullifying the employment restriction on private enterprises.

35. This figure appears extraordinarily high and is to some extent misleading: it appears to include some large co-operatives, many of which are still in the process of restructuring their ownership along lines common in market economies.

36. *Survey to ascertain the development problems of the small and medium private sector in Romania,* mimeo, National Agency for Privatisation, June, 1992.

37. In addition, the NAP will act as a regulator.

38. A brewery was privatised by public offering of 49 per cent of its shares, the remainder being held for a strategic investor. A textile factory was sold to employees with a majority to a foreign investor.

39. It should be stressed that the sale of plant and equipment up to a certain value has been permitted since late 1990.

40. In addition, RAs and CCs may not bid for other firms or assets.

41. This is one example of the tendency, also seen with price controls, to search for a ``normal rate of return''.

42. In particular, taxes are reduced by 50 per cent if profits are reinvested in Romania or by 25 per cent if the firm meets certain criteria to export, import, carry out domestic procurement or create jobs. Such regulations could actually discriminate against domestic entrepreneurs and lead to round-about FDI.

43. The official statistic refers to commitments and actual investment. The cumulated balance of payments figures are substantially less than the sum mentioned in the text.

44. Up until December 1990, the banking system comprised five institutions but there was not a two-tier banking system.

45. Banks had very little freedom of action at this time.

46. In April 1991, two further laws established the regulatory framework giving the NBR substantial independence from the government, though it remains accountable to the Parliament.

47. This has been further undermined by the extensive resort to subsidised credits. For example, from July through December 1992 the Romanian Agricultural Bank (RBA) made loans at an average rate of 48.5 per cent, while paying between 42 and 44 per cent for deposits. However, only about 15 per cent of RBA loans are financed with customer deposits; the rest comes from NBR refinancing or interbank lending from the CEC. The interest rates on these funds were 70-80 per cent and 65 per cent over the period, respectively, except for NBR special refinancing credits, which carry a 15 per cent interest rate.

48. As part of their universal banking privileges, banks may also acquire up to 20 per cent of a non-financial firm's shares.

49. In two tranches – one of 265 billion lei and later in 1990 one of 15 billion lei.

50. This has since been increased to 90-95 billion lei.

51. The debt write-offs improved banks' debt average equity ratio from 20:1 to 12:1, still above international standards.

52. The NBR took measures, including the imposition of reserve requirements, to offset the expansion. Moreover, it also provided for interest on the special credits at market rates, eliminating what may have been an incentive for late payment.

53. At the time of writing, Rafirom, a state holding company responsible for oil imports, could not import oil because it lacked enough domestic currency to deposit against letters of credit – a result of 82 billion lei in arrears on the part of its customers. This occurred despite 12.2 billion lei in special, low-interest credits that Rafirom received from the NBR in August 1992 to relieve the financial blockage, which it has not been able to repay.

54. Food prices in peasant markets were liberalised in early 1990, accompanied by a devaluation of the lei to 21 lei/dollar.

55. Originally raw materials' prices were to have been liberalised more rapidly than prices of final consumer goods; the November 1990 stage reversed this.

56. For details, see Demekas and Khan, "The Romanian Economic Reform Programme", *IMF Occasional Paper 89,* November 1991, pp. 19-20.

57. Allocation was, and still is, performed by the Directorate for Industrial Correlations on the basis of annual production plans submitted by enterprises. The system of allocation is different for state-owned firms and for private firms. The former apply directly to their branch ministry, providing their annual plan and information on stocks. Private firms apply through local committees. If approved, firms receive their supplies every three months either from local warehouses belonging to the state distribution system or directly from the manufacturer. Resale is prohibited.

58. For example, the administered prices for raw materials were not high enough to cover the domestic cost of extracting coal and iron ore or of smelting copper, lead and zinc. These producers received temporary subsidies. Reduction of producer subsidies was a condition of IMF support for the stabilization programme which went into effect in April 1991.

59. One consequence was an *ex-post* government decision to reimburse producers locked in to fixed prices for the losses caused by the depreciation: Decision 329 in June 1992 subsidised importers with domestic supply commitments existing as of November 1991 for the difference between the price fixing exchange rate of 180 lei/dollar and the actual interbank rate. These payments, which were not on-budget, included 36.1 billion lei from the stock revaluation account in 1991 and 123 billion lei in 1992 from the government's gold revaluation account at the NBR. In addition, the increased lei value of foreign liabilities has also been subsidised.

60. A commitment was made to the World Bank to increase the price of natural gas 10 per cent per quarter in real terms until parity is reached.

61. It may also have led to imports being deferred and thus one factor influencing the surprisingly good balance of payments figures by mid-year.

62. In the meantime the interbank exchange rate had further depreciated to 430 lei/dollar although the foreign exchange market still did not appear to clear.

63. The trade share controlled by the private sector has grown quite dynamically: by the end of 1991, private exports and imports accounted for 19 per cent and 16 per cent, respectively, and this has since grown to around 25 per cent at the end of 1992.

64. Romania became a contracting party to the GATT in 1971. It signed the protocol of accession with a non-discriminatory import commitment and in 1973-1974 introduced a customs tariff. However, the convertible currency trading partners did not consider it effective because of quantitative restrictions and central planning. Consequently, contracting parties were permitted to impose ''specific restrictions'' under the provision for trade with state traders. Following the widespread systemic changes of the last three years, Romania requested a working party to re-negotiate its terms of accession in February 1992. Moreover, Romania also plans to accede to the codes on subsidies and public procurement.

65. Important features included: generalised exemptions from tariffs that had been granted to state enterprises for production inputs were rescinded; and the highest tariffs, with many items falling in the range 0-20 per cent, were substantially reduced.

66. This is permitted under GATT obligations on balance of payments grounds.

67. OECD calculations based on the UNCTAD data bank of NTMs.

68. Chapter 5, Article 36, Law 15/1990 prohibits: a) monopoly pricing and dumping; b) discriminatory pricing between customers; c) tying of contracts. Enforcement is left to private agents and no penalties are specified.

69. Interestingly enough, this law is enforced by local Chambers of Commerce.

70. The aggressive cancellation of old debts is often argued as important but these proposals concern a *one-time* cancellation of *all* debts and the simultaneous recapitalisation of the banking system. See, for example, D. Begg and R. Portes, *Enterprise debt and economic transformation: financial restructuring in Central and Eastern Europe,* London 1992, and also P. Bofinger, *The experience with monetary policy in an environment with strong microeconomic distortions,* Frankfurt, 1992.

71. In an effort to avoid reporting arrears to the Ministry of Finance and Economy, the duration of negotiated inter-enterprise credits appears to have increased.

72. In its Aide-Mémoire of October-November 1990 the Bank staff wrote: ''The Mission is seriously concerned that the complex mixture of free and controlled prices will lead to substantial economic distortions and that full price liberalisation may become politically more difficult to implement with time''. See Council for Reform, Bucharest, 1991, *op. cit.*

73. The budget balance remained substantially in surplus at 8.4 per cent of GDP, but estimated including the losses of state firms showed a significant deficit (as quoted in Montias *op. cit.*).

74. Between November 1990 and April 1991, the Romanian government in co-operation with the IMF developed a full-fledged macroeconomic stabilisation programme which ran from April 1991 to March 1992. The programme was renewed again in the spring of 1992.

75. Note that the budget authorities used a forecast of 89 per cent inflation for 1992, in terms of October 1991 prices. While the NBR and Ministry of Finance share their forecasts, there is no indication that the government uses a consensus forecast for monetary and fiscal policy, quite the contrary. Romanian authorities publish various inflation forecasts, but it is often difficult to discern whether these are year-on-year, December-on-December, or some mix of the two, which is often the case.

76. This in any case may have been fortunate, since liberalisation in the face of poor enterprise financial discipline may have resulted in excessive interest rates.

77. In August the NBR increased the spreads to four percentage points and abolished the system in September.

78. In the third quarter of 1991, credit even fell in nominal terms; in September alone it decreased from 806 billion lei to 750 billion lei.

79. The temporary injection of credit was around 1.2 trillion lei, but after mutual payment of debts was reduced to 400 billion lei.

80. The question of how to interpret money and credit aggregates in an economy in transition is totally unsettled. The basic insight that inflation can only be sustained if the money supply grows to accommodate it must apply to all economies, and money growth is linked to credit expansion via certain accounting identities. However, the precise relationship between different definitions of money and credit and inflation are not known, and are perhaps very unstable. In the text, the sum of domestic credit expansion and gross inter-enterprise arrears is taken as one rough indicator of inflation potential. This may not be fully warranted in theory, because inter-enterprise arrears, unlike bank credit, do not give rise to money creation. However, it seems that inter-enterprise arrears can serve to increase the velocity of circulation of money by providing a mechanism for economising on cash balances, and to this extent need to be explicitly taken into account when assessing the stance of monetary policy. Some analysts have suggested that the net stock of inter-enterprise arrears should be added to bank credit for purposes of defining an appropriate credit aggregate. The argument for this is that net arrears define the amount of bank credit that would have to be injected into the system in order to clear all arrears. It is not clear, however, that the capacity for inter-enterprise arrears to permit an acceleration in velocity is better captured by this measure than by gross arrears.

81. *Monetary policy in the transition period,* mimeo, National Bank of Romania, Bucharest, 1992.

82. Of the 200 billion lei, only 100 billion in credits were actually extended before the programme lapsed.

83. According to Montias, *op. cit.,* the exchange rate was derived from the average cost in lei of exports necessary to acquire one dollar. The spread of actual exporters was quite wide, the extreme being 65 lei/dollar.

84. Foreign exchange auctions had begun in February so that the dual exchange rate system *de facto* began at that time.

85. The authorities recognised that a dual rate was a temporary expedient and expected to reunify the rate eventually – the crisis merely precipitated the inevitable.

86. In this period, multiple currency practices were effectively re-introduced. In an effort to stem capital flight, the NBR issued regulations that excluded foreign exchange bureaus from the interbank market, and placed limits on purchases of foreign exchange by individuals through foreign exchange offices. This action led to a widening of the spread between the bureau and inter-bank rates.

87. The interbank auction did not eliminate excess demand. An auction system was adopted which searches for the exchange rate at which the largest number of bids for dollars can be executed, given the offer. For details, see *Romania Economic Newsletter,* Vol. 2, No. 2, September 1992.

88. In a series of interviews in the Romanian paper *Adevarul* (15 January 1993), the NBR governor explained that the freeze of the exchange rate at 430 lei/dollar in the last months of 1992 was the price that the NBR accepted to pay for political and social stability.

89. The policy rationale appears to have been to allow the exchange rate to devalue with shocks to the price level caused by the gradual, staged pattern to price liberalisation. In between price shocks, the exchange rate was to be stabilised to avoid hyperinflation in the context of a monopolistic economy.

90. Over the whole period the difference between the official and the "market" exchange rates has been very large (Figure 4). In 1991 the premium averaged around 300 per cent, but fell to 50 per cent in 1992.

91. The definition of the general government budget deficit includes the state (federal) budget, the local government budgets, and extra-budgetary funds, the most important of which are the unemployment and pension funds. Until 1990 these were included in the state budget deficit. In the 1991 and 1992 state budget these have been accounted for separately.

92. In July and November 1990, the turnover tax was extended to all goods and services and the number of rates greatly reduced. The profit tax was reduced and the wage fund tax was replaced with an individual wage tax. These changes resulted in large declines in revenues, but were partly offset by significant increases in both customs duties and social security contributions so that revenues only declined by 17 per cent net. Reforms continued in 1991, when the number of brackets and rates for most of these taxes were greatly simplified (*e.g.* the profit tax has only two rates, 33 and 45 per cent).

93. Firms pay a total of 66 per cent taxes on the wage bill, split between employer and employee contributions. Paid directly by the firm as a percentage of the wage bill are: social security: 27.5 per cent; unemployment tax: 5 per cent; risk and accident insurance: 2 per cent; Research Fund: 1 per cent. Additionally, firms pay taxes on employees of: 25 per cent wage tax (average); 1 per cent unemployment tax; 3 per cent supplemental pension contribution.

94. In OECD countries, payments by firms of taxes on behalf of employees would not be considered as a contribution by enterprises to the budget: questions of tax incidence arise. The text is not concerned with incidence but with dependency of the budget on the financial condition of enterprises: employees' "contribution" or not, tax arrears are significant.

95. The Department of Accounting within the Ministry of Finance sets accounting standards – no independent standards board exists, and consequently all accounting is based on tax accounting. Statements about accounting practices in Romania are at best tentative as practice appears to vary widely across firms. The MOF monitors compliance, but is unable to audit all 6 000-plus state firms annually, and independent audit firms are still in their infancy.

96. In late 1992, in preparation for the transfer of commercial companies from direct state ownership to ownership by the SOF and POFs, fixed assets were revalued again, but the old asset values are still being used for depreciation calculations. This valuation will not be permitted to affect depreciation calculations until 1994 because of its potential revenue effects. Estimates by the Ministry of Finance indicate that if there is 100 per cent pass-through – something which the cost-plus price controls almost ensure – this could raise prices by 37-40 percentage points. Whether this could indeed occur depends on monetary and wages policy.

97. Anecdotal evidence suggests that some firms are even still carrying stocks from as long ago as 1988.

98. Estimates of the size of unrealised losses arising from failure to value stocks at the minimum of market value are impossible to make with the level of information available.

99. Extrabudgetary funds had a flow surplus of 238 billion lei – the 1993 budget projects a surplus of 148 billion lei, not adjusted for inflation.

100. A simple numerical example: At the beginning of 1992, assume that bread production costs were 50 lei per loaf, and the subsidised price was 25 lei, for net subsidy of 25 lei or 50 per cent of costs. The government raises the price of bread to 35 lei (two rounds of 25 per cent cuts), but in the meantime production prices go to 100 lei, so the actual subsidy increases to 65 lei or 65 per cent of cost.

101. The other funds are supplemental pension, research, health, and education.

102. In 1991, the forecast for average unemployment was 6.6 per cent when in the event it barely reached 3 per cent by the end of the year. The initial 1992 budget set targets for unemployment expenditures, and a small deficit on this account based on average unemployment rates of 8.1 per cent. This rate was not reached until mid-November, and the estimated annual average will be about 6.1 per cent.

103. The other account is the inventory or stock revaluation account. Of the total inflows in 1992 of 37.4 billion lei, 10 billion were transferred to local budgets and 5 billion were used to cover interest payments to commercial banks on bad loans to state enterprises that the government assumed in 1991.

104. Every time the assets are revalued with a depreciation, a corresponding special deposit is created. According to Romanian law, these funds can only be used at year-end and for non-inflationary purposes.

105. According to Ministry of Finance sources, the impact on payments by state importers was 400 billion lei in 1992.

106. The foreign currency inflows, primarily World Bank funds, over the whole period amount to some 2.7 billion dollars. Romanian authorities estimate that as much as 90 per cent of the foreign currency was allocated for consumption rather than developmental purposes.

107. Treasury notes/bonds issued in 1992 amounted to 34.8 billion lei, of which 31.5 billion lei were issued directly to banks.

108. These are negotiable bearer bonds, in denominations of 25, 50 and 100 thousand lei with a maturity of 2-3 years, though they appear to be redeemable in 6 months at the option of the purchaser. They carry a minimum interest rate of 50 per cent, which matches the deposit rate offered by the Savings Bank, and are indexed on a 1:1 basis with the NBR refinancing rate. One potential obstacle is that these bonds are in direct competition with the deposits at the Savings Bank but offer a more attractive package, providing disincentives for the Savings Bank to market them. So far, they are only being sold at the Bucharest branch of the Savings Bank, despite expressions of demand in the countryside.

109. There are legal restrictions on the financing of the budget deficit through the banks. Nevertheless it appears that ways were found in 1992 for the savings bank to support the budget.

110. In March, wages were increased by 15 per cent with the intention of lifting real wages to 70 per cent of the October 1990 level.

Summary of Discussion

On 26 March 1993 a seminar was held in the Organisation's headquarters to discuss the economic situation in Romania, based on a draft Economic Assessment prepared by the OECD Secretariat. The discussion covered a wide range of issues, although there was a tendency to focus on progress made in structural reform, and its relationship to the limited effectiveness of Romanian stabilization policy to date. This report is not a record of proceedings, but it summarises salient points made in the draft Assessment and during the discussion. Additional information and data were presented by Romanian participants, and were incorporated into the revised Assessment.

The Assessment noted that Romania has in fact undertaken major reforms over the past three years, albeit starting from extremely difficult initial conditions. A stabilization programme has been pursued in such a manner that targets for monetary and fiscal restraint have been achieved. Growth of nominal wages has been contained. The legal framework for a market economy is largely in place. Reforms in the fiscal and financial systems have been enacted and new policy instruments developed. A corporate profits tax has been implemented and decentralisation of central government powers to lower, autonomous levels begun. Agricultural collectives have been dismantled and the basis for private ownership of land re-established. Foreign trade has been substantially liberalised. The framework for a mass privatisation programme has been established. Starting from an extremely small base, private sector activity is once more emerging.

Notwithstanding these achievements, the Assessment noted that the economic situation remains critical – structural reform is not sufficiently advanced to provide the foundation for a sustained recovery. Most of the industrial sector remains under state ownership and is not subject to financial discipline – these enterprises have been insulated from pressures to adjust through incomplete price liberalisation, the accommodation of inter-enterprise arrears, and provision of subsidised credit. Incomplete price liberalisation has permitted some parts of the bureaucracy to continue with direct administrative intervention in the economy, and has allowed these elements, often in conjunction with key interest groups, to slow or reverse implementation of some reform measures at the first sign of pathological market responses. All of these factors have undermined policy credibility and limited the effectiveness of stabilization policy. As a result, production has continued to fall and inflation remains high and volatile. The authorities have not been able to establish confidence in the currency, so that the market exchange rate has been repeatedly devalued. The budget has been balanced based on inflation-related taxes on enterprises which are serving to decapitalise them. Fiscal expenditures have shifted heavily towards social protection and subsidies, replacing government investment which has collapsed. Thus, "gradualism" in Romania has meant support for the existing enterprises and mix of output, with the effect of prolonging the duration of output decline.

The Romanian participants in the seminar felt that the Assessment was realistic, but exaggerated the extent to which controls and administrative allocation remain in the Romanian economy. They emphasised that initial conditions inherited from the Ceausescu regime were extremely difficult, but that significant progress had been made in creating government institutions appropriate to a market economy. Still, the Romanians recognised that the record of macroeconomic stabilization was at best mixed and felt that the draft Assessment's call for more coherence between structural reform and stabilization was consistent with the new 1993 economic programme.

The Romanian participants stated that the government remained committed to stabilization. Fiscal policy will aim to restrain deficits through controlling tax evasion and introducing a value-added tax in July 1993. A free floating exchange rate will be maintained with intervention confined to attempts to build up foreign exchange reserves. The government was committed to a tight but "appropriate" monetary policy – including positive real interest rates – and would cease to accommodate inter-enterprise arrears. Wage policy would be improved by partial indexation of wages to improvements in productivity.

The Romanian participants emphasised the need to introduce competition and financial discipline in the economy. In support of this the government plans to introduce a competition law to Parliament and to improve public tendering procedures. An emergency financial restructuring programme will be implemented in which bad loans to 112 of the biggest loss-making state enterprises would be removed from bank portfolios, after which banks would be recapitalised and appropriate prudential regulations promulgated. One plan under consideration would convert inter-enterprise arrears into negotiable securities. Financial discipline would be enforced through a bankruptcy law, soon to be submitted to Parliament, supported by management contracts which will be issued as part of the privatisation programme. Private investment funds and secondary markets for enterprise shares will be stimulated. As these changes take effect, remaining controls on prices of inputs and firm profit margins will be lifted gradually.

In their questions and comments, seminar participants focused on anticipated difficulties in implementing the government's programme, especially in the area of structural reform. In particular, key aspects of the programme awaited parliamentary approval. Powerful resistance could also be expected from some government agencies which had not yet "internalised" such goals as price liberalisation. Financial discipline would remain extremely difficult in the absence of appropriate pricing signals. Seminar participants warned that enterprise restructuring may prove difficult under incomplete price liberalisation and with an accounting system that does not allow discrimination between profitable and unprofitable enterprises. Reforms in these areas could not be delayed pending demonopolisation, which will take some time to complete.

Some participants believed that the Romanian bureaucracy had placed increasing reliance on administrative measures rather than market mechanisms. These covered the gamut of economic policy, especially in the foreign exchange market, with the result that there was now a large gap between official and parallel rates, which undermined the credibility of exchange rate policy. This raised the concern that if transparent, market-oriented, measures were not taken now, the pain of economic contraction would be prolonged, raising the risk of subsequent political backlash.

Several questions from participants reinforced the importance they attached to achieving coherence, transparency and credibility in the implementation of economic reform. Among the points raised were: What is the outlook for enactment of the various laws before Parliament that would be required before the government's new programme came to fruition? Is the programme coherent and how would it be implemented in an appropriate sequence? For example, doesn't the current policy mix result in incentives to run down the capital base of industry, while allowing enterprises to continue subsidising inflated payrolls? Why are consumer prices to be liberalised first, when controls on input prices and margins are far more important to achieving market clearance? Aren't the series of *ad hoc* administrative measures creating an inordinate lack of transparency, even for the government officials responsible for implementing policy? Concerning credibility, how could the government assure that the current effort to deal with inter-enterprise arrears would be the last? (Past accommodation had led to a monetary expansion on the order of 50 per cent of GDP). How could commercial paper be issued against arrears which looked very nearly uncollectible?

A number of questions were dealt with at some length by the Romanian participants. The credibility of the policy regarding inter-enterprise arrears would be enhanced by the fact that this time the sources, rather than the symptoms, of the problem were being addressed: the principal loss-makers were being singled out for special action. The intention to provide limited support to some enterprises from budgeted resources would make enterprise subsidisation more transparent than at present. Moreover, a lot had already been achieved: the stock of arrears at the end of 1991 amounted to 19 per cent of GDP, but by the end of 1992 had fallen to 6.5 per cent of GDP. On exchange rate policy, progress had been made, including unification of official rates in December of 1991; policy had shifted frequently since then, but authorities were now agreed on the need to stabilize the exchange rate in real terms at the current rate, to stem inflation. There is no administrative allocation of foreign exchange. If the government stabilization policies for 1993 were to be threatened, fiscal policies would be tightened. In particular, rates for value-added, profits and excise taxes would be raised and social expenditures reduced through targeting.

With respect to the implementation of large-scale privatisation, Romanian participants acknowledged that the government's current programme was not yet approved by the Parliament. The number and nature of state enterprises exempted from the privatisation process was under review; in any event these enterprises were to be subjected to improved control through promulgation of management contracts. Plans were being drawn up to provide special incentives to private sector firms through credits and credit guarantees, exemptions from the profit tax, and continued subsidisation of credit in the near term. Nonetheless, subsidised credits had diminished in real terms. In retrospect, gradual adjustment of prices had entrenched inflationary expectations. There was still a need to improve the transmission of macroeconomic constraints to the microeconomic level.

When considering the overall balance of the discussion, several widely supported points stand out. Seminar participants agreed that policy implementation had been poor at times and that there were serious problems requiring urgent attention. There was agreement that the new government programme sought to deal with most of the issues identified in the Assessment and participants hoped that it could be successfully implemented. All (including the Romanian participants) realised that this was not assured and would require a major effort by the government.

The Romanian Accounting System: False Profits and Firm Decapitalisation

In preparing this study of Romania, the OECD encountered persistent complaints that state enterprises were suffering from severe shortages of liquidity. These liquidity shortages were repeatedly attributed to tight credit policies by the NBR, and are viewed by most Romanian observers as the explanation for the explosion of inter-enterprise arrears in 1991 and again in 1992. While monetary policy has been relatively tight, with some exceptions, the magnitude of complaints and arrears appears to be disproportionate. At the same time, it is striking that the Government of Romania has been successful in keeping the budget in near balance despite the dramatic fall in GDP. Most surprising was the sustained level of profit taxes, and, by inference, profits, despite the fall in industrial production of 26 per cent in 1991 and 14 per cent in 1992. Enquiry by the OECD suggests that the enterprise accounting system could conjointly explain these phenomena. There were slightly conflicting descriptions of the accounting system[1] but from analysis of the accounts of firms under the supervision of the Ministry of Industry (MIND), an internally consistent understanding emerged.

Income is accounted for on a mixed cash and accrual basis. Production is divided into five categories. These are: 1) final product delivered and cashed; 2) final product delivered and not cashed; 3) final product without a market; 4) final product invoiced but not delivered; and 5) final product not sold. The first and third categories are counted as income, the other three are not and are accumulated in inventories. Categories 1 and 3 combined accounted for 74 per cent of total final production for MIND firms in the first semester of 1992, and 86 per cent of total income. Category 2 corresponds to accounts receivable, and is analogous to inter-enterprise credits, including arrears. This item is included in total inventory figures, giving a distorted picture.

Costs are accounted for on something approaching an accrual basis – they are counted whether paid for or not – but only the costs of producing categories 1 and 3 above are measured in total costs for tax purposes.[2] While firms are permitted to mark down unsold inventories, it appears that this is either not done at all, in which case losses are never realised, or only done at year-end.[3] The value of increased inventories in semi-finished and finished products is not included as a cost. Thus, for the sample, recorded costs were only 74 per cent of total costs (net of taxes, taxes not included, and inventory gains). This method of accounting places enormous pressures on firm liquidity and cash flow, especially for industries with long production times or that carry significant inventories. These effects are compounded in a period of declining sales, accumulating inventories and high inflation.

Romanian firms use historical cost accounting for inventories, or FIFO. As is well known, in an inflationary environment this artificially inflates profits. More importantly it leads to the decapitalisation of the firm and chronic illiquidity, as the firm is forced to replace inventory at higher cost. These effects are significantly magnified in an environment of high inflation and real inventory accumulation, as characterised Romania in 1991 and 1992.

Table I.1 presents OECD estimates of the influence of inflation on decapitalisation for Romanian firms for 1991 and 1992. To calculate the effect on cash flow,[4] real average total

Annex I

Table 1. **Cash flow effects of inflation accounting**

	1991	1992
Average industry final stocks, deflated (bn lei)	101.7	
1992 ratio industry to total stocks	7.3	
Estimated average total stocks, deflated (bn lei)	743.4	1 574
PPI inflation (Dec./Dec., per cent)	234	102
Negative cash flow (bn lei)	1 739	1 605

Sources: Ministry of Economy and Finance, OECD calculations.

inventories were calculated by deflating nominal monthly inventories by the producer price index. This figure was then multiplied by the annual PPI inflation rate to arrive at the effect on cash flow. In 1991, total inventories were inferred from data on industrial final goods inventories, based on the ratios found in the more complete data available to us for 1992. 1992 inventory and PPI data were only available through October. At the time of writing, PPI data was not available for November and December 1992 – it was assumed that the PPI and nominal inventories increased by 10 per cent in each month. While these calculations are admittedly quite crude, the size of the negative flow is so enormous as to leave little doubt as to what has occurred in Romania. There has been an enormous decapitalisation, which readily explains the illiquidity experienced by industrial firms.

As discussed in Chapter IV, depreciation is grossly understated in Romanian accounting because of the undervaluation of fixed assets and excessively long asset lives. Estimates of the size of this distortion can be made from the MIND data set. Data from the first semester of 1992 show that firms under the supervision of the MIND charged 68.3 billion lei in amortisation on average fixed assets of 2 232 billion lei, (implying an average life of 32.6 years) of which 70 per cent was charged as costs. Adjusting only the asset life to 15 years, total depreciation would increase to 148.8 billion lei. Charged at 70 per cent this would have decreased gross profits for this sample from 116 to 60 billion lei, and profit taxes from 52.2 to 27 billion – nearly 50 per cent. Combined with realistic values for fixed assets, appropriate accounting of depreciation would probably eliminate profits, and therefore profit taxes.

The Romanian authorities have recently revalued fixed assets as part of the transfer of ownership from the government to the state and private ownership funds. This revaluation has not been allowed to affect depreciation for tax purposes; this will be delayed until a new accounting system is introduced in 1994. The reticence of the authorities to raise depreciation allowances appears to be based not only on budget considerations but on its supposed direct effect on inflation. The Ministry of Finance estimates that a pass-through of higher depreciation allowances, if permitted, would increase the price level by 20 per cent in 1993. This is a misunderstanding of market pricing, whereby sunk costs such as depreciation have no direct effect on pricing – the assumption behind the calculations in the previous paragraph – but Romanian firms may not respond in this manner, given the lack of financial discipline and competition. In the case of strict markup pricing, permitting appropriate depreciation would substantially alter relative prices between capital – and non-capital – intensive firms.

Notes and references

1. Based on interviews with an independent economist, the former chief accountant for a large state enterprise, and the Deputy Director for Accounting in the Ministry of Economy and Finance.

2. Except possibly for wages. We received conflicting information on whether wages were accounted for proportionate to sales. For the firm sample, wages were a sufficiently tiny percentage of total actual costs, about 5 per cent, that it was impossible to distinguish from the data which version was correct.

3. In CEEC countries profit taxes are calculated monthly. This is despite the fact that the accounting systems are widely acknowledged to be deficient.

4. Cash flow is equal to profits at historical cost (HCA) plus amortisation, less the inflationary bias in profits induced from FIFO accounting, less real inventory accumulation. The calculation in Table I.1 covers this third effect only.

Agricultural Reform

Rural life and agriculture play a much more important role in the Romanian economy than in any of the other CEECs. The large fertile plains in the east and south, particularly the Danube basin, give the country a comparative advantage in cereals and oilseeds, particularly wheat, corn and sunflowers. Historically Romania served as the breadbasket for the Ottoman Empire, and, after independence in the 19th century, for Western Europe. As recently as the Second World War 75 per cent of the labour force was engaged in agriculture. This declined dramatically as a result of the Communist emphasis on heavy industrialisation. Still, in 1991, agriculture accounted for 27.5 per cent of total employment and for 18.5 per cent of gross domestic product.[1] Forty-five per cent of the population still lives in rural areas, though many of these are elderly, often single women.

Under the old regime, agriculture was used to cross-subsidise consumption and industry. These policies were reinforced by the drive for current account surpluses in the 1980s, so that agriculture was starved of resources and investment. Production peaked in 1986 and dropped steadily thereafter, the index of agricultural production falling 14 per cent by 1989, with the largest drop coming in meat production. Romania remained a net food exporter through most of the 1980s, largely achieved by a savage drop in food imports and domestic consumption: food imports were compressed from 485 million dollars in 1986 to 270 million dollars in 1989. Per capita calorie consumption fell from 3 259 in 1980 to 3 057 in 1985 and 2 949 in 1989.

Restoring agricultural production and launching agricultural reform were an immediate priority for the new government in 1990. Reversing the decline in food consumption and ensuring adequate food supplies was seen as a humanitarian and political necessity. As in many countries, agricultural and rural life are considered to be the cradle of Romanian civilisation, so that restoring peasant production was viewed by many as essential to the cultural renaissance.

Prices in peasant markets were liberalised almost immediately in early 1990 and formal state monopolies in buying of agricultural commodities and supplying of inputs were quickly abolished. An initial land privatisation programme in early 1990 was followed by the almost complete privatisation of agricultural co-operatives. To protect consumers and provide for the needs of the population, price controls and subsidies on essential consumer food items were maintained or introduced in 1990, and these have been removed only gradually. Despite these steps, domestic production of key consumption items like bread, milk and cooking oil have been insufficient to meet domestic demand at controlled prices. Significant expenditures of scarce foreign exchange on food, fodder and fertiliser imports have not resolved the problem: for some key food items Romania is still best characterised as a shortage economy. Government officials and the domestic press regularly portray agriculture as in a state of near crisis. The crisis is ascribed to shortages of various inputs and problems in adjusting production, input delivery and marketing systems to a decentralised market with many small producers, rather than to the distortionary effects of subsidies and price controls.

This annex begins with a description of the organisation of production, including land tenure, the provision of inputs and the system of marketing. Agricultural pricing and the role of government intervention, particularly subsidies, is then discussed and domestic prices compared to world levels. Privatisation and restructuring, pricing, subsidies, and competition are finally drawn together to explain the performance of agriculture since 1990.

Land Privatisation

Under the Ceausescu regime, agriculture was nearly totally controlled by the state under the direction of the Ministry of Agriculture and Food Industries (MAFI), with 95 per cent of arable land under state ownership.[2] Farming was organised in the form of 411 state farms and 4 500 co-operatives – the result of forced collectivisation completed in 1962 – which were subsequently consolidated to 4 226 by 1989. State farms, which accounted for 18.6 per cent of agricultural area, were larger – twice the size of co-operatives – averaging about 5 000 hectares per farm. They were more capital-intensive, owning 59 per cent of the fixed assets and accounting for half of all land under irrigation.

Initial privatisation – the allocation of 0.5 hectares to each person – was followed up by the Land Law, number 18-1991, which covers the privatisation of agricultural co-operatives. Implementation is under the control of local commissions headed by mayors. The privatisation policy had a goal of creating a small-holding peasant class, essentially recreating the agricultural structure of pre-World War II agriculture (without the large estates). To achieve this, a maximum of ten hectares per household was set, which applies to the total holdings of any household within all of Romania.

The basic principles of land privatisation are restitution to those who contributed land to co-operatives, and land grants (usually smaller) to others who have worked in agriculture but lack restitution rights. Agricultural specialists and workers in co-operatives who had not originally contributed land were permitted to make application for land grants of up to 10 hectares out of unclaimed land controlled by the commissions, with specialists receiving priority.[3] If no land is available for specialists and workers, the local commission can affect a proportionate reduction in the size of holdings to be restituted. State farms were converted into commercial companies, and claimants on land taken by state farms were given shares in these companies in proportion to their restitution claims. Communal grazing lands seized by state farms or co-operatives were restituted to the appropriate commune.

Implementation of the Land Law has been beset by the size of the problem and bogged down in the detailed issues of restitution. Over 6 million applications were received, though many were from heirs to the same household. Commissions have been poorly staffed and subject to manipulation and favouritism by powerful local interests.[4] They have had to adjudicate competing claims which are complicated by the law and the fragmented nature of ownership. For example, the law ensures restitution of the same mix of land, but ownership prior to collectivisation was often divided into many separate plots – little pieces of arable land, pasture, orchards, and vineyards. As a result, eighteen to twenty million separate parcels were to be distributed.[5] Cadastral records in many regions were organised by the name of the owner, rather than by plot, making title searches laborious. Issuing title may require surveying as many as ten plots.

As a result of privatisation, about 70 per cent of all agricultural land and 82 per cent of arable land is now in private hands in one form or another.[6] By the end of 1992 nearly all legitimate claimants had been issued certificates of ownership or vouchers, which are not equivalent to actual title.[7] Cadastral surveys are just now being completed so that only around 100 000 titles have been issued, out of 2.3 million total, with another 200 000 in process. Livestock has been privatised to a much smaller extent and varies widely across species: state agricultural commercial companies (former state farms) hold 19 per cent of cattle, 50 per cent of pigs, 15 per cent of sheep and goats, and 50 per cent of fowl.

Privatisation has caused average plot size to fall to a little less than two hectares of arable land and three hectares in total. Many recipients no longer work in agriculture, a consequence of the transfer of population into industry and urban areas: their holdings account for one-third of total area. Another quarter of total area has been restituted to the elderly.[8] This pattern of small holding is found also with livestock: the privatisation of most dairy cows has resulted in an average herd size of a little over two.

The Romanian government has sought to mitigate the effects of fragmentation through voluntary associations, essentially recreating co-operatives while trying to avoid the onus associated with that name. Under the Land Law, co-operatives were to be dissolved under the supervision of a liquidating commission, and required to dispose of their non-land assets within nine months of dissolution. Co-operative members were given the option of forming either agricultural associations (unincorporated), societies (incorporated), or to become independent farmers. Where the members chose one of the first two paths, ownership rights were to be allocated based on the relative size of restitution claims. Individuals opting out of association were to be given creditor status, and those opting out of societies were to be allocated inefficient land not included in the societies. Where co-operatives were completely dissolved, non-land assets were to be auctioned off with the proceeds divided amongst the members proportionately.

Agricultural societies and associations have been increasing steadily in number, but comprise a much smaller percentage of cultivated area than did co-operatives under the old regime (Table II.1). By year-end 1992 nearly all co-operatives had converted to societies, and the number of associations had increased sharply, but land controlled by these entities accounted for only 25 per cent of total area, implying many farmers have as of yet chosen not to join. Regarding the state farms, the share of private ownership ranges from 20-70 per cent in individual firms, with 140 having a majority of private ownership. State farms (including animal breeding) will be privatised as part of the mass privatisation programme beginning in 1993, discussed in Annex III.

It is unclear what has happened to the surface area which is not accounted for by state farms, societies or associations. This may represent private farmers who have chosen to opt out of societies and associations and are operating individually or are part of societies and associations currently being formed.[9] Alternatively, there may remain co-operatives that are still operating as such, *de facto* or *de jure,* no doubt partly as the transfer of land is still being completed. There are numerous reports that, to avoid fragmentation into small plots, the MAFI has pressured farmers to remain in or join some form of association, through a combination of incentives and penalties. These include the possible loss of financial interest in former co-operative assets; being held liable for a share of co-operative debts, whereas those shouldered by societies and associations were forgiven; allocation of the worst quality land; and lack of access to the numerous state agricultural subsidies, as well as to credit, inputs and machinery services (partly because delivery and distribution systems are not geared to small farmers).

Unless government pressures to create societies and associations are successful, consolidation of holdings through market processes will be inhibited by constraints on land usage and transfer built into the Land Law. The law places a maximum of 100 hectares on the holding or leasing of any family. It prohibits recipients of non-restituted land (*e.g.* collective members who did not contribute land in the initial collectivisation) from selling their land for ten years. Selling or leasing of land must be approved by the local commission and are subject to a series of rights of first refusal:[10] co-owners, neighbouring owners, and then the Rural Development Planning Agency. Exchanges of land where one of the parties is a juridic person requires approval by MAFI or the Ministry of the Environment. All owners of arable land are required to maintain it under cultivation, subject to fines, and can have their land expropriated after two years of non-cultivation.

In 1992, many small holders chose to lease their land, a consequence of the fact that many newly restituted holders are urban dwellers or elderly. In most cases lessors were state farms or Machine and Tractor Stations (SMTs). Lease arrangements ranged from all work being done by the lessor, a system especially popular with urban owners, to provision of certain services, machinery services being the most common. Most contracts stipulated payment in shares of output rather than

Table 1. **The structure of agricultural organisation**

	Number	Total area (000 hectares)	Percentage share	Average size (hectares)
Pre-reform, 1989				
State farms	411	2 976	20	7 241
Co-operatives	4 260	8 685	58	2 039
Private farms		3 189	21	
TOTAL		14 850	100	
Year-end, 1990				
State farms		2 804	19	
Co-operatives		6 526	44	
Private farms		5 420	37	
TOTAL		14 750	100	
Year-end, 1991				
State farms	411	1 919	13	4 669
Agricultural societies	2 250	1 095	7	487
Agricultural associations	8 338	1 226	8	147
Individual farms and agricultural groups in formation		7 997	54	
Individual farms	2 000 000			
Agricultural groups	2 411			3 317
Communal		2 561	17	
TOTAL		14 798	100	
April 1992				
State farms	411	1 919	13	4 669
Agricultural societies	3 270	1 482	10	453
Agricultural associations	11 057	1 574	11	142
Individual farms and agricultural groups in formation		7 262	49	
Individual farms	2 000 000			
Agricultural groups				
Communal		2 561	17	
TOTAL[1]		14 798	100	
Year-end, 1992				
State farms	411	1 919	13	4 669
Agricultural societies	4 050	1 915.9	13	473
Agricultural associations	11 499	1 791.7	12	156
Individual farms and agricultural groups in formation		6 610	45	
Individual farms	2 000 000			
Agricultural groups	1 515			
Communal		2 561	17	
TOTAL[1]		14 798	100	

1. Assumed to be the same as end-1991.
Source: Ministry of Agriculture.

cash. These arrangements allowed small holders access to needed services and capital; and to share risk while at the same time avoiding being committed to selling their crops to state integrating units at low prices (discussed below). This leasing was technically illegal: no land leasing law exists[11] and farmers without clear title are incapable of signing valid formal contracts.

Agricultural marketing and supply

Under the communist regime, agricultural marketing and supply were totally integrated and controlled by the MAFI. Inputs were supplied by the Division of Material Inputs through distribution centres in each district (judet), and seeds were supplied from the seed monopoly. Output was then marketed by state monopolies, often vertically integrated from purchasing at farm-gate to ownership of retail outlets. Machinery services were traditionally provided by state enterprises known as SMTs, which owned almost all tractors, seeders, combines and harvesters not owned by state farms.

Reform of agricultural supply and marketing has been driven by conflicting state objectives. On the one hand, the government has publicly stated goals of decentralisation, elimination of state intermediaries, and the privatisation of retail outlets. On the other hand, the state has wanted to retain some control of the production structure to ensure consumer protection and provision of essential consumption. As in the case of non-agricultural industry, the former objectives have generally been sacrificed to the latter.

State agro-industry firms have been converted to commercial companies, with the important exception of the *régie autonome* ROMCEREAL (RC). Except in the case of fruits and vegetables and some dairy products, the state distribution and marketing system is largely intact and operates as a monopoly under central direction. RC alone controls the distribution of 50 per cent of domestic wheat production, plus imports, and serves as the principal intermediary between oilseed producers and crushers/refineries. State firms still account for 90 per cent output for the latter.

State-owned marketing and food-processing firms maintain their market power through their role as "integrators". Integrators are firms which are permitted to advance inputs and financing in exchange for forward purchase contracts of agriculture crops at fixed prices. Integrators are able to offer inputs like fertiliser and finance at greatly reduced rates because of their preferential access to state subsidies. State farms are also classed as integrators, allowing them to benefit directly from credit subsidies and buy at subsidised prices. The same pattern exists with SMTs. Though state farms and SMTs have been converted to state-owned commercial companies, they continue to operate as local monopolies with integrator status. Over 50 per cent of tractors are owned by the SMTs with another 23 per cent owned by state farms. Small private farms have limited access to alternative sources of inputs because of their small size, price discrimination, and because private alternatives do not exist (for reasons discussed below). Thus, despite privatisation of most agricultural land, farmers still must enter into supply contracts with the state sector if they are to gain access to modern inputs such as certified seed, animal feed, vaccines and chemical fertilisers.

Price reform

During the Ceausescu regime state farms and co-operatives were required to sell their production to the state purchasing fund at fixed prices, which remained unchanged from 1982 to 1989. Prices were set so that agriculture subsidised other sectors of the economy (*e.g.* wholesale and retail prices were nearly equal so that all marketing costs were absorbed by the food industry). As a result, agriculture produced at a loss, accumulating debts with the banking system which were periodically forgiven.

The pattern of price reform has been similar to that in non-agricultural products. Prices in peasant markets were liberalised almost immediately after the Revolution, and two-tier pricing permitted. Prices on most retail food items were liberalised in November 1990 except for a list of

22 essential items which were subject to subsidies and whose prices were fixed. This was reduced to five products in mid-1991, and binding price ceilings were substituted in April 1991 and converted back to controls in May 1992, but the net effect has been the same. For all of the period until September 1992, retail price controls existed on bread, cooking oil, milk products, sugar, and basic meat products. Directly or indirectly, agricultural inputs into these products accounted for one-third or more of the total area cultivated, and probably a similar amount of private consumption expenditures. As of September 1992, after the latest round of price increases and subsidy cuts, formal retail price controls only remained on bread and milk.[12] However, many retail food items sold in state-owned stores now appear to have fallen under the system of supervision and controls on margins detailed in Chapter III, so that in practice these prices are still not determined by market forces. A recent case illustrates the results of this policy: retail food outlets were not stocking edible oil because of low profit margins, creating shortages, while at the same time there was nation-wide surplus at the wholesale level, some of which was in fact exported. The government responded by requiring state-owned stores to purchase edible oil to sell to the population.

In Romania, price controls at the retail level imply controlled prices at the farm-gate and various wholesale levels because of the system of subsidies, limits on mark-ups, and monopolies over distribution. The best example is bread and wheat (wheat accounted for 25 per cent of all cultivated area in 1989-91). Bakery prices for standard bread are fixed in nominal terms (16 lei in November 1991, 18 lei in February 1992, 24 lei in May 1992, and finally 40 lei in September 1992), as are subsidies. Bakers are limited to a 10 per cent margin on costs (raised from 5 per cent prior to November 1991) in order to be able to receive subsidies, and since flour prices account for the vast bulk of input costs, this effectively limits prices bakeries can set for flour. Flour mills purchase from RC at fixed sales prices, permitting them about a 13 per cent profit on sales. The operating margins of RC are controlled because of its monopoly status, and are in fact set at less than 1 per cent. As a result, farm-gate prices are determined. Retail, wholesale and farm-gate price determination operate similarly for oil and oilseeds, milk and butter, and meat products through September 1992. It is unclear whether the recent round of retail price liberalisations has altered wholesale and farmgate price-setting appreciably.[13]

The effect of price and margin controls is that prices for controlled products like wheat tend to be below international prices, as shown in Figure II.1. This has made it difficult for RC to purchase wheat on the open market from those farmers who have declined to participate in forward purchase agreements. In response, the government has banned the export of bread grain and flour, along with rice, sugar and milk, though bans have been difficult to enforce. The government has attempted to enforce wheat sales to RC through a number of methods. Majority-owned state farms have been required to sell to RC, though whether this applies to in-kind earnings from leasing arrangements is unknown. As noted earlier, subsidised credit, fertiliser and other inputs are used to induce sales to RC in exchange for purchase of output at the fixed price. The monopolistic position of RC and the flour mills, and their low profit margins, have made the development of private sector competition unprofitable and nearly impossible. Peasant markets cannot compete because they are either too small or unsuited to products requiring processing. Unable to export and with the size of private markets limited, farmers who have not switched to other crops instead store grain in expectation of increases in state prices: construction of private storage has been booming, some observers suggest that private agents now hold almost all grain stocks, especially corn. At the margin the government is faced with importing wheat at world prices or paying domestic producers, while the farmer holds an asset which is appreciating at the rate of devaluation, earning a healthy nominal return.[14]

Prices of the principal agricultural inputs (feed, fertiliser, seeds and mechanical services) are in theory negotiated but in practice tightly controlled and are set well below international market prices (decisions 464/1991 and 53/1992), as a subsidy to agriculture. This is accomplished by fixing raw material prices and margins for processors.[15] Feed prices are at one-fifth of world levels and fertiliser have not moved in over two years, despite their heavy reliance on imported energy (natural gas) and other inputs. Mechanical services are underpriced because of fixed margins and inaccurate accounting of capital costs: lack of proper inflation accounting or depreciation measures.

**DOMESTIC PRICES OF WHEAT AND
CORN IN COMPARISON TO WORLD PRICES**

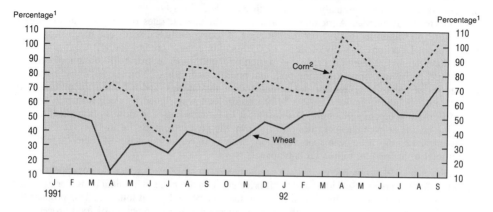

1. Romanian wholesale prices for wheat and corn were converted to dollar equivalents and expressed as a percentage of monthly U.S. export prices; for the dual exchange rate period (April-November 1991), an average of free and official rates has been utilised (see Figure 6 for details) and for other periods the official rate has been used.
2. Romanian domestic prices for August-October 1991 estimated by OECD.
Sources: World Bank, US Department of Agriculture, OECD statistics and OECD calculations.

Subsidies and support to agriculture

Along with energy, agriculture is the most subsidised sector of the Romanian economy. Retail food subsidies to consumers were initially put in place with the first round of price reform in November 1990, covering a broad range of 22 essential goods. They covered only products sold in state stores at controlled prices. This list was reduced to five items in July 1991 – bread, meat, sugar, cooking oil and milk. In February 1992, subsidies were increased again following the devaluation of November 1991, but were reduced in May 1992 by 25 per cent and by the same percentage again in September, with subsidies eliminated on oilseeds, sugar and meat. Total price subsidies to agriculture in 1992 were nearly 200 billion lei, or over 3 per cent of GDP.

The nominal cuts in subsidies have in reality been less than stated. Bread subsidies increased in February 1992 from 37.5 per cent of retail cost to 90 per cent, so that the cuts of May and September leave subsidies still at 56 per cent of retail prices. The elimination of retail subsidies on low-quality meat was accompanied by the introduction of direct subsidies to producers on all meat; therefore total subsidies increased. The total cost of meat subsidies, including imported fodder, was 63 billion lei in 1992, over 1 per cent of GDP. In the case of milk, subsidies actually increased because of the effects of inflation on the farm-gate prices.

Subsidies are substantial on inputs as well. Fertilisers were granted an on-budget subsidy of 6.9 billion lei in 1991, and have been provided with imported inputs at well below cost. The 1991 budget also included 3.3 billion lei for covering increases in material and capital expenditures. Direct credits of 6 billion lei for autumn 1990 and 1.8 billion lei for spring 1991 to agricultural works, and 1 billion lei in investments were financed directly by the budget in 1991. In 1992, the budget included subsidies of 41.8 billion lei to produce fertilisers and veterinary drugs. Preliminary reports indicate that 73.4 billion lei has been included in the proposed 1993 budget for payment of production bonuses.

Budget subsidies were supplemented by large amounts of low-interest credit in 1991 and 1992. Fifty billion lei in low-interest financing was made available to agriculture in 1991. Seventy percent of these credits were eventually funnelled through RC. In 1992 the NBR made refinancing available to the Romanian Agricultural Bank (RBA) at interest rates of 13 per cent to support agriculture: 80 billion lei in 1992 for the purchase of fuels, fertilisers, seeds and mechanical work (Government Decisions 565/1991 and 54/1992). Including these credits, the RBA extended over 241 billion lei in preferential credits to agriculture and food industry: 70 billion directly to agriculture, 25 billion for restructuring pork and poultry husbandry, 20 billion for financing winter inventories of food, 30 billion for potato and fodder inventories, and 6 billion for purchases of agricultural machinery. In July 1992 a $100 million loan was signed between Romania and the World Bank to promote agriculture. Disbursement to farmers has been slow as farmers anticipate receiving credits at even cheaper rates directly from the government. So far in 1993, 15 billion lei in low-interest credits have been approved, along with a project for purchases of chemical fertilizer, with a total of at least 50 billion lei anticipated.

Subsidies and low-interest credits are supplemented in other ways which do not appear on the budget or NBR accounts. Subsidies and retail price controls are fixed in nominal terms for extended periods of time, implying declining real prices in the face of triple-digit inflation. This protects the budget at a cost of undermining incentives to producers and the profitability of food processors.

The Government's policy for prices of annual crops varies over the course of the year. It has been geared on the one hand towards minimising prices within the current market, but on the other indicating an acceptable price level for the new harvest. The effect of keeping prices very low and then moving them up sharply at the end of the marketing year effectively shifts part of the consumer subsidy from the budget to marketing and processing firms.

Finally, continuing with previous practice, outstanding agricultural debts of 65 billion lei, dating from the 1984-88 period of controlled prices, were erased in 1990 (by Decree 43/1990) and offset against bank deposits of the government. In 1992 another 111 billion lei of debts incurred in the period 1989-90 (Law 12/1992) were written off. The current financial status of agricultural industries and farmers is unknown.

The performance of agriculture since 1990

The index of agricultural production fell modestly in 1990 to 97.5 per cent of 1989 levels before growing by 0.5 per cent in 1991. However, the share of agricultural value-added in GDP rose 15 per cent in 1990 due to a decrease in inputs such as fertilizers and energy and perhaps by a reduction of animal herds. In 1992 output collapsed largely as a result of a drought: cereal production was down 55 per cent year-on-year and sugar fell by 65 per cent, but production of fruits and vegetables increased significantly. From the government's perspective, the situation is poor: the private sector is not producing the mix of products the government desires, especially cereals, oil and sugar,[16] and state integrators are unable to purchase sufficient quantities at government procurement prices to ensure food delivery at subsidised retail prices.[17]

The transfer of land to peasants has compounded the problems caused by mispricing by affecting the crop mix and the proportion of output marketed. The transfer of land ownership to independent farmers, by allowing for a market determination of production, caused a dramatic change in the composition of output. As Figure II.2 shows, under the old regime private farmers produced almost entirely corn. State farms and co-operatives had a diversified production, which was ordered by the plan regardless of prices or productive advantage. They produced a large number of cash crops like sugar beets and sunflowers, for which they accounted for almost all of production.

A crude estimate of the effect of privatisation on the total output mix can be calculated by holding the 1989 product mix constant for each type of ownership, but changing the ownership proportions. This method predicts a 65 per cent drop in wheat acreage, a 70 per cent increase in

Annex II, Figure 2. **AGRICULTURAL PRODUCTION BY FARM OWNERSHIP TYPE**

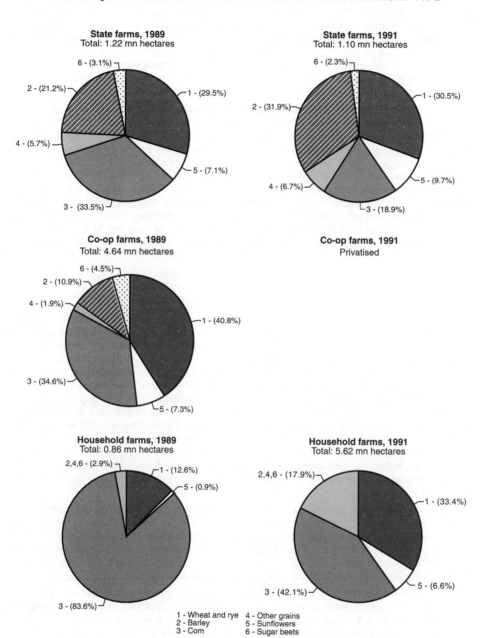

State farms, 1989
Total: 1.22 mn hectares

6 - (3.1%)
2 - (21.2%)
1 - (29.5%)
4 - (5.7%)
5 - (7.1%)
3 - (33.5%)

State farms, 1991
Total: 1.10 mn hectares

6 - (2.3%)
2 - (31.9%)
1 - (30.5%)
4 - (6.7%)
5 - (9.7%)
3 - (18.9%)

Co-op farms, 1989
Total: 4.64 mn hectares

6 - (4.5%)
2 - (10.9%)
4 - (1.9%)
1 - (40.8%)
3 - (34.6%)
5 - (7.3%)

Co-op farms, 1991
Privatised

Household farms, 1989
Total: 0.86 mn hectares

2,4,6 - (2.9%)
1 - (12.6%)
5 - (0.9%)
3 - (83.6%)

Household farms, 1991
Total: 5.62 mn hectares

2,4,6 - (17.9%)
1 - (33.4%)
5 - (6.6%)
3 - (42.1%)

1 - Wheat and rye   4 - Other grains
2 - Barley   5 - Sunflowers
3 - Com   6 - Sugar beets

Sources: National Commission for Statistics, OECD calculations.

109

corn acreage, and a 68 per cent drop for other cash crops. Comparing 1992 acreage and 1991 production with 1989, (1992 production results are suspect because of the severe drought which affected yields) indicates that planting of wheat and rye acreage has fallen steadily – 38 per cent by 1992 –, and production was down by 37 per cent through 1991 (Table II.2). Corn production rose by 40 per cent through 1991, and production of the key cash crops – oil seeds and sugar beets – fell 20 and 30 per cent, respectively.[18] The strength of fruit and vegetable production, even with the drought, is attributable to the fact that these items can be sold on local peasant markets and are not subject to price controls.

The transfer of land to peasants also affected the proportion of output marketed. It allowed for the dramatic decompression of peasants' consumption from the forced extraction and redistribution of the agricultural surplus which occurred under the old regime.[19] Many peasants appear to have adopted a ''safety-first'' strategy of guaranteeing their own needs by growing a diversified mix of crops for own consumption before worrying about market production. This strategy has been reinforced by the lack of any tax payments on the part of private agricultural producers, further diminishing the need for interaction with the monetary economy. There is clearly a redistribution of food consumption away from urban consumers to the peasantry, exacerbating the differential in favour of peasants who have always eaten better, even in the worst years. Thus the recorded drop in agricultural production (and the attendant decline in per capita consumption to 2 850 calories in 1992) is probably mismeasured because much of peasant production (and consumption) goes unrecorded.

Assessment

The privatisation of agriculture has meant farmers can respond to profit incentives and to relative prices, however distorted these might be. They are now capable of shifting production into more profitable crops or converting raw products whose prices are regulated into unregulated final commodities. The relative prices that farmers now see as a result of government-induced distortions have reinforced the peasants' traditional emphasis on corn and away from wheat, sunflowers and to a lesser extent sugar beets.[20] Export prohibitions and low state procurement prices, instead of securing a high rate of domestic supplies, have had the opposite effect (*i.e.* they have provided incentives to farmers to move into other crops). In other commodities like milk and butter, price controls mean milk is largely unavailable in private markets. Farmers convert milk and butter into cheese which is in plentiful supply. The disincentives provided by distorted relative prices are compounded by farmers' desire to avoid being locked into unprofitable, or less profitable forward contracts with state-controlled integrators. In sum, these policies have limited earnings of foreign exchange, reduced the profitability of farming, and therefore lowered the availability of funds for investment in agriculture.

In an ironic twist, the government's policies on wheat echo those of the Ottoman Empire when it controlled Romania, with the same effect. Starting back in the late 16th century, the Ottomans began to enforce a trade monopoly on those parts of Romania under its control. Wheat exports to other countries were forbidden: ''The obligatory sale of wheat to Constantinople, for example, helped ensure the success of corn when it was introduced. More and more corn was grown for domestic consumption precisely because it was not required by the Porte''.[21]

There has been a strong tendency on the part of the government and Romanian agricultural experts to treat the problems of the last two years as if they were technical, a result of shortages of inputs like diesel fuel, fertiliser, tractors, spare parts, and credit. It is alleged that the new farmers lack experience and sufficient social capital, generating declining yields[22] (*e.g.* about one-third of recipients of reconstituted land were non-farmers).

It is true that technical problems have contributed to declining agricultural production. The problems of state farms, and probably some agricultural societies with similar factor endowments and production patterns, are different from those of independent farmers. The difficulties experienced by state farms are similar to those of heavy industry, for the same reasons: they are quite

Table 2. The structure of agricultural production

	Total crops	Total cereals[1]	Wheat and rye	Barley[2]	Corn	Oil seeds	Legumi-nous crops	Sugar beets	Potatoes	Vegetables	Fodder crops
1989											
Arable land (000 hectares)	n.a.										
Arable land under crops (000 hectares)	9 847	6 027	2 359	768	2 733	1 072	311	256	351	253	1 149
Total production (000 tonnes)		18 379	7 935	3 436	6 762	1 034	256	6 771	4 420	3 727	n.a.
Average yield per hectare (tonnes)		3.0	3.4	4.5	2.5	1.0	0.8	26.5	12.6	14.7	n.a.
1990											
Arable land (000 hectares)	9 450										
Arable land under crops (000 hectares)	9 402	5 704	2 298	749	2 467	655	130	163	290	216	1 962
Total production (000 tonnes)		17 174	7 379	2 679	6 809	739	112	3 278	2 831	2 358	n.a.
Average yield per hectare (tonnes)		3.0	3.2	3.6	2.8	1.1	0.9	20.1	9.8	10.9	n.a.
1991											
Arable land (000 hectares)	9 410										
Arable land under crops (000 hectares)	9 197	6 049	2 217	1 018	2 575	643	81	202	235	195	1 552
Total production (000 tonnes)		19 307	5 559	2 951	10 497	823.4	79	4 703	1 873	2 214	n.a.
Average yield per hectare (tonnes)		3.2	2.5	2.9	4.1	1.3	1.0	23.3	8.0	11.3	n.a.
1992											
Arable land (000 hectares)	9 299										
Arable land under crops (000 hectares)	8 907	5 774	1 476	628	3 337	807	69	180	219	223	1 323
Total production (000 tonnes)[3]		12 289	3 228	1 678	6 828	n.a.	n.a.	2 877	2 602	2 632	n.a.
Average yield per hectare (tonnes)		2.1	2.2	2.7	2.0	n.a.	n.a.	16.0	11.9	11.8	n.a.

1. Includes oats, sorghum and rice.
2. And two-row barley.
3. Total 1992.
Sources: National Commission for Statistics and OECD calculations.

input-intensive, particularly in the use of energy or energy products. The examples are numerous: state farms rely heavily on chemical fertilizers; they make extensive use of irrigation relying on energy inefficient pumps; and, they fatten animals using a feed mix containing too little protein, resulting in conversion ratios half of those in the West, so that value-added in meat is probably negative. Like heavy industry, state farms are having difficulty sustaining production in the new economic environment.

The solution for state farms has been to both directly allocate and to subsidise scarce supplies of credit and inputs to them. Massive credits – nearly 5 per cent of GDP – have been made available: diesel fuel has been directly allocated, fertilizer subsidised, and fodder has been imported and subsidised. This approach has not worked. Shortages result from controlled prices because subventions are inadequate to cover costs: prices on fertilisers are so low that the state cannot afford to supply natural gas at subsidised prices during the winter, so that enough fertiliser must be produced and stored by November for spring. Diesel fuel allocations were not used for harvesting but for much more profitable transport activities. The MAFI is a clear example of regulatory capture by organised special interests, notably the Democratic Agrarian Party (PADR).[23] By and large, subventions have encouraged rent-seeking by state farms and agricultural societies, as the recent investigation into misappropriation of subsidised credits and state investment funds indicate.[24]

The problems of independent producers are different, and largely a result of deliberate policy choices. The key problem is a result of selecting restitution as the method of privatisation – newly privatised plots are too small to be efficient, especially given the existing stock of machinery. Delays in issuing of certificates of ownership, and the total lack of progress on issuing titles,[25] have created uncertainties over future ownership so that a high proportion of land is not being cropped amidst a myriad of legal cases. Lack of clear ownership and legal limitations on land sale and leasing have inhibited consolidation into more productive units.

The major instrument of Romanian agricultural policy, credit subsidies, has not reached small farmers because access has been tied to sale of output to state procurement in order to reduce the independence of private producers in responding to market signals. It is not even clear if credit shortages are a problem: despite such allegations, many cereals farmers have found sufficient money to finance the construction of storage space, which is used to hold cereals until RC prices improve.

Agricultural policies have failed fundamentally because they have been halfway, legislating restitution without ensuring sufficient resources for cadastral surveys, issuing titles and dispute resolution; creating a nation of tiny plots while discouraging consolidation into more efficient size; privatising land ownership without privatising or creating competition in agricultural supply or marketing; and not allowing prices to move and affect relative profitability and investment. The development of private agricultural input supply and food processing industries has been completely inhibited by the ineligibility of private firms for state funds and subsidies, and the fact that profit margins are strictly controlled, so that rates of return are too low to attract private investment. Investment by farmers in livestock, building and equipment is inhibited by low prices for crops and lack of titles with which to secure loans.

For agriculture to be a success story, the Romanian authorities need to go more than halfway and complete the process they have started. This means liberalising prices of inputs and outputs, allowing for relative profitability to determine investment and provide for investment funds, and eliminating agro-industry monopolies through privatisation and an active competition policy. Recently, as part of its mass privatisation programme in 1993, the government announced that agro-industry and SMTs would be priority sectors for privatisation to stimulate competition and production. This appears to be a good start.

Notes and references

1. These figures no doubt underestimate the size of the agricultural sector as there are an enormous number of small plots and non-market production which are not reflected in official statistics.

2. Unless otherwise noted, all historical figures are for 1989, the last year of the old regime. From Cristian Risavi, *et al., Romania: Overview of Agricultural Restructuring and Transition to A Market Economy.* FAO/NITRA Workshop, Rome, May 1992.

3. Law 18, Articles 17, 20 and 95. Unconfirmed reports indicate that in many localities agricultural specialists have often been allocated the full 10 hectares allowed, putting them in powerful positions in their multiple roles as MAFI employees, advisors to societies and associations, and independent landowners. Families wishing to establish themselves in farming can also make applications for land in areas with labour shortages and excess land. Local public servants can request allocations of 0.5 hectares.

4. "... Petre Marculescu, the Minister of Agriculture, said that a check... had shown that the work of the county and local commissions for the application of the land law was very poor. One of the reasons why property certificates were no longer being released and the land law no longer being applied was that many local commissions had disbanded after most of their members had solved problems of personal interest". Radio Free Europe *SWB* EE/W0255. Munich. 5 November 1992, p. A/6.

5. Local commissions and surveyors have obvious incentives to slow down the process to maintain employment for as long as possible.

6. There has also been the transfer of about one-third of the land controlled by state farms to communal or private use, almost all of which is grazing land.

7. "... Until October 31, 1992 about 4.7 million vouchers (92.4 per cent of total number of vouchers) have been issued and there are still 385 thousand vouchers to be issued; out of the total area of some 9 million ha about 7.8 million ha (86.4 per cent) have been assigned to a number of 3.9 million persons out of a total of 5.1 million persons (77.2 per cent)." *Agricultural Policies, Markets and Trade,* OECD, 1993 (forthcoming).

8. The rural elderly present a long-term problem for the government, and a potentially large claim on future government expenditures. Currently there are over one million pensioners from former agricultural co-operatives. Their monthly checks average around 500 lei, a tiny fraction of the minimum wage.

9. Given the numerous articles complaining about fragmentation of agriculture into small plots, it is likely that a lot of farmers are operating independently.

10. The World Bank's Country Economic Memorandum on Romania (December 1991) notes: "The law requires that all agreements for subsequent transfer cannot be legally executed until a chop from the land commission has been received, usually within thirty days. During this period, the commission can either approve the agreement, or else choose to substitute the state for the purchasing party and buy the land rights at the price agreed between the two parties, or – should the agreed compensation exceed limits established in the law (which reportedly are quite low) – the commission can invalidate the agreement and attach the land for ultimate disposal by the state."

11. A leasing law has been drafted and was being debated in Parliament as of this writing. One of the issues of debate was whether a leasing law was appropriate when most farmers still do not have title to their land.

12. Sugar and oil were still being sold at subsidised prices because the population was owed these products for several previous months.

13. Meat price determination has differed slightly. Prior to November 1991, prices were "negotiated", based on state estimates of normal costs plus an acceptable rate of return. This process was formalised thereafter with fixed prices, which effectively lowered prices.

14. In 1992, because of the lagged nature of price setting coupled with the exchange rate depreciation, world wheat prices were 120-130 dollar/tonne versus 93 dollars (exchange rate of 430/dollar and price of 40 000 lei) from RC, despite the worst drought in modern Romanian history. This inspired farmers, evidently even some farms with state interests, either to export wheat, wait for higher prices, or retain cereals for animal feed. The government response was the imposition of strict export prohibitions, followed in August by a decision requiring that "all commercial companies in which the state has a majority holding, research institutes and stations must sell their whole 1992 wheat crop to ROMCEREAL". Eventually, in early October the government raised prices, but by only 12 per cent; this was ineffective in releasing peasant stores to the market at the time of writing.

15. For feed, this is a derivative of RC fixing the farm-gate cereal and oilseed prices. Fertiliser receives both explicit subsidies as well as inputs imported by the government and provided below cost.

16. "By the decentralisation of the economy as a whole, in this transition period there are wrong correlations between the social demands and the structure of agricultural production. In 1991 we had insufficient crops of sugarbeet, sunflower, soya, but larger ones of corn, vegetables and melons" (Risavi, *op. cit.*).

17. Under the old regime farms were required to keep a certain number of livestock, which resulted in old and poor-quality animals being maintained. After the Revolution, these animals were slaughtered, as well as an indeterminate number which were "spontaneously" privatised.

18. While this example is meant to be indicative, the comparison is affected by the fact that state farms and co-operatives substituted away from corn to compensate and offset the peasants' preference for it, a shift already in evidence in 1990.

19. It appears that large parts of peasant production are no longer marketed. One anecdote from a dairy association near Brasov indicated that they are now producing four times as much milk, but are still marketing the same amount.

20. Corn has the additional advantage of being easily convertible into meat. The same is true in crops like oilseeds, whose production cycle is a very close substitute to corn and where on-farm storage is more difficult to construct because of volatility, production has dropped so dramatically as to require rationing of 1 liter per person. As early as 1990 Michael Montias had noted that distorted pricing was leading to a drop in sugar beet and sunflower production. See Montias, "The Romanian Economy: A Survey of Current Problems", *European Economy*, No. 2, 1991.

21. Vlad Georgescu, *The Romanians,* Ohio State University Press, 1991. p. 26.

22. Interestingly, while yields in wheat, rye and barley have all fallen, yields in corn have increased steadily since 1989.

23. The PDAR has a large membership among agricultural specialists and tends to represent their interests. Agricultural specialists occupy a unique place in Romanian agriculture: many still work for the state; at the same time they are often significant landholders as a result of privatisation, and have become members of agricultural societies and associations. In a press release in late 1992, the PDAR cited the lack of diesel fuel, fertiliser, credits, and animal feed as causing food shortages. They requested that the government roll back price increases in agricultural inputs and meat resulting from the devaluation (from 220 to 430), which are "giving rise to speculation and unjustified dissatisfaction". In 1993 the president of the PDAR announced "the only way to save this year's crop ... 300 billions of lei [of low interest credits] would be needed for the completion of the farming work during this spring." *Cronica Romana,* 11 February 1993.

24. An investigation was launched in October 1992 into fraudulent applications for state investment subsidies and the misuse of state funds for importing sugar and manipulating government sugar stocks for private profit.

25. To try and speed up the process, in late 1992 the government issued decisions 728 and 730 to improve the quality of local commissions by, among other things, attracting more specialists in cadastral surveying and topography.

Annex III

The Plans for Large-Scale Privatisation

This Annex discusses the future of the Romanian privatisation programme, following on the discussion of privatisation to date contained in Chapter III. It focuses on the mass privatisation programme scheduled to begin in mid 1993 which aims to privatise all commercial companies (CCs) within seven years. The programme will be administered through six new institutions: five private ownership funds (POFs), representing the public's 30 per cent share held in the form of vouchers; and a state ownership fund (SOF), controlling 70 per cent of the shares on behalf of the central government. Vouchers representing some 30 per cent of the value of the assets, but issued to the public at a nominal fee, will play an important role in the privatisation.

These two sets of institutions will play a dual role in the mass privatisation programme. They are privatisation agencies as well as active owners.[1] The legislation authorizing mass privatisation has left unclear some responsibilities of the multiplicity of institutions – including Ministries – particularly for restructuring. The nature of relations between the Ownership Funds and enterprises is not yet clarified: the Funds will have to monitor enterprise management for what could be an extended period, depending on the pace of privatisation. Depending on the precise rules and incentives adopted, the programme could either significantly accelerate the transition to a dynamic market economy, or become captive to interest groups and perpetuate enterprise dependence on the state, delaying the establishment of market relations.

Starting in late 1992, the state began transferring 70 per cent of the share capital of each of the 6 280 CCs covered in the privatisation to the SOF and the remaining 30 per cent to the five POFs.[2] This process is expected to be completed by April 1993 but delay is being encountered in establishing clear land titles.[3] During the coming months, there will be a series of shareholders' meetings at which the SOF will be represented by the existing State Representative Council (SRC) for each enterprise. The SRC will then be dissolved and Administrative Councils will be constituted for each enterprise comprising three to nine members. Generally speaking, the SOF and POFs will divide members according to their stakes (70/30). In the absence of agreement between the SOF and the POFs, the former is clearly the dominant actor. The only restriction in the law on the use of this power is that the SOF cannot oppose the distribution of dividends amounting to at least 50 per cent of an enterprise's profit. The relations between the SOF and the POFs are to be regulated by shareholders' agreements between them which will be crucial for the path of the privatisation programme and the management of enterprises.

The SOF is an independent public institution run by a board appointed by the government, the President and the Parliament for fixed five-year terms. However, the board members are subject to recall by the appointing body.[4] The role of the SOF is to develop and implement annual privatisation programmes leading to complete privatisation within seven years. To this end it will: exercise the customary rights and obligations as a shareholder; define minimum performance criteria for the CCs and the dividend policy; and take measures in co-operation with each POF for the privatisation, restructuring or liquidation of the CCs. In addition, the SOF is also empowered to grant credit to facilitate privatisation.

115

The five POFs are joint stock companies, the shareholders being each of the 16.5 million Romanian citizens over the age of eighteen on 31 December 1990 who have taken up the offer of certificates of ownership – around 15.5 million by the close of subscriptions in December 1992.[5] The Funds are run by Administration Councils (not to be confused with those for enterprises) proposed by the government, appointed by the economic commissions of the Parliament, and approved by both chambers of Parliament, which may also revoke these appointments. The POFs are envisaged to operate for five years from the date of the enactment of their founding legislation; after that they will be converted into ordinary closed-end mutual funds. At the beginning of 1993, the POFs were scarcely functional. In carrying out their activities the Funds may use specialised firms for restructuring, valuation and sale of the enterprise. No shareholders meeting of the POFs is envisaged for the first five years.

The Law specifies the objectives of the POFs to include:

- carrying out profitable activity to the benefit of the Funds' shareholders, in order to increase the value of certificates (dividends are not to be distributed for three years but capitalised);
- developing methods to permit Fund shareholders to exchange their certificates for shares in the companies themselves;
- selecting CCs in which the Fund is a shareholder for privatisation through the sale of the enterprise's shares according to the Shareholders Agreement with the SOF;
- portfolio management and new investment to maximise the market value of certificates.

A special feature of the POFs is that they have the right and the obligation to preserve and increase the value of certificates; in this respect they may repurchase their own certificates. The certificates of each Fund are tradeable but the authorities have shown great concern that their value could fall precipitously. To avoid this, the Funds are supposed to engage in repurchase of their certificates "at the market price". Moreover, to determine the uses to which certificates may be applied (see below), the Funds' Administration Council must publicly announce every quarter their unit value. The relation to the market price is unclear. In any case, "market price" is ambiguous in a situation where the Fund is supposed to influence it directly. Situations can also be imagined where the Fund cannot simultaneously repurchase certificates and at the same time carry out "restructuring" and other operations.

Governance rights and responsibilities are being created and allocated by distributions of enterprise shares between the five POFs, and by shareholder agreements between the SOF and the POFs. The law foresees co-operation between the SOF and the POFs, as defined in a Shareholders Agreement for each enterprise, in carrying out the measures initiated by them for the speeding up of the privatisation process. Where there is a conflict between the SOF and a POF, the NAP will adjudicate. Proposals by the NAP in late 1992 foresaw a systematic distribution of these rights roughly according to firm size (Table III.1).

A primary goal in allocating enterprises to POFs has been to establish them as regional leaders.[6] Furthermore, for the operation of the voucher scheme it was also necessary to ensure that the Funds, at least initially, be roughly equal in profitability levels, capital and the number of employees.

To meet these objectives, enterprises were divided into four groups: regional, specific, strategic and banks. The first group included agriculture, construction, and commerce. All enterprises from these industries in a given region have been allocated to their local POF (*i.e.* it holds 30 per cent of the shares in all these enterprises). The second group includes construction materials, pharmaceuticals, textiles and clothing, tourism, non-ferrous metals and electronics. For a given industry in this group, the enterprises shares were allocated to just one POF (*i.e.* they are also specialised by sector, if necessary across regions). The third group, strategic, includes chemicals, ferrous metallurgy and machinery.[7] For the strategic sectors, individual firms are allocated to different POFs, but industries are split across POFs. For the banks, the 30 per cent shareholding will be equally spread across all Funds (*i.e.* each will receive 6 per cent of the shares of each bank.) The grounds for this allocation differ. In the case of the first two sectors, it was a consequence of

Table 1. **Companies in the mass privatisation programme**

Field of activity	Commercial companies [1]				
	Capital (billion lei)	Total	Small	Medium	Large
Mining, resources	11	72	29	39	4
Industry	782	1 919	443	1 162	314
Agriculture	181	1 259	442	773	44
Communications	0.3	6	4	2	0
Transportation	85	500	253	230	17
Construction	64	451	229	195	27
R & D, education	95	349	263	73	13
Trade	74	662	287	356	19
Financing – banking	38	18	6	2	10 [2]
Services – incl. tourism	110	1 044	612	397	35
TOTAL	1 443	6 280	2 568	3 229	483

1. Small – less than 50 mn lei.
   Medium – between 50 mn and 500 mn lei.
   Large – more than 500 mn lei.
2. Includes the state savings bank, which has since been removed from the programme.
Source: National Agency for Privatisation.

their poor financial condition and future prospects: it was not considered desirable to load down any one Fund with such a large shareholding. In the case of banking, it was a justified fear of directed bank lending. This risk is however greatest for the SOF: pending resolution of this crucial issue (see below) the distribution of shares in banking to the SOF has been delayed.

Enterprises classified as small (2 568 enterprises though the figure appears to have been reduced recently to 2000) are to be privatised in 1993 by regional commissions comprising the NAP, the SOF and the POFs. The preferred method will be via management and employee buyouts (MEBO) but if that fails, the enterprises will be auctioned. To make the former path attractive, a 10 per cent discount on shares will be made and credit will be available from the SOF to be repaid in either monthly or half-yearly instalments. For this reason, as well as the fact that it is organisationally better developed, the SOF is likely to dominate the process.

For medium-sized firms,[8] the proposal at the end of 1992 was that the SOF would delegate full powers, via a shareholder agreement, for privatisation (and presumably other management powers) to the relevant POF. However, at the beginning of 1993, the SOF made it clear that the methodology had not been developed, and that privatisation would proceed on a case-by-case basis.

Under the proposals in effect at the end of 1992, the SOF would thus be left with around 800 large and medium-sized firms "which need considerable investment to be restructured, based on sectoral strategies and case by case privatisation strategies". Statements in early 1993 indicated that it was hoped to privatise four to five large firms in 1993.

The role of certificates

All eligible citizens had the opportunity between June and December 1992 to receive "Certificates of Ownership", comprising shares in each of the five POFs, for a small fee – 100 lei, which was less than 1 per cent of the average monthly gross wage. By December, about 15.5 million had made use of the opportunity. The certificates are tradeable – although foreigners are not permitted to participate – and a flourishing trade developed in them as early as August 1992. By January 1993, the black market price was between 1 500 and 7 000 lei – a very small fraction of the estimated "nominal value" of the enterprises with respect to which these certificates represent ownership claims.

The bearer certificates have a variety of uses covering both the distribution of wealth and the process of privatisation. With respect to the former, the certificates may be retained and after three years the holder may be able to obtain dividends. The certificates may also be traded and funds may establish a floor price for repurchase or for use in privatisation.

The certificates will be used in three ways in the privatisation process. First, they may be used to purchase the shares of an enterprise from the POF which owns the 30 per cent stake, at which point the Fund annuls those certificates. The law sets no limits on the number of certificates that any individual can use in this way; the Administrative Council of the Fund is free to decide. The procedure for changing the certificates for shares will be determined by the POFs. With an established "market price" for the certificate, the question will come down to the valuation of the enterprise shares held by the POF, with all its attendant problems.[9] Small companies are excluded by law from having their shares sold in this manner.

Second, management and employees engaged in a buy-out of a small company may use certificates from all the five POFs to purchase an enterprise's shares from one POF. When the sale price is greater than the collective value of the certificates, cash will also be part of the transaction as well as credit from the SOF.[10] The modalities of how the certificates are to be returned to the respective Funds for cancellation, compensation, or both, are still to be finalised. What is interesting about the scheme in this instance is that it is used to promote "insider" privatisation.

Third, when the SOF is engaged in selling shares in one of its (large) enterprises, the certificates pertaining to the particular POF which holds the other 30 per cent of the enterprise's shares may be presented in order to receive a 10 per cent discount on the public offering price.[11] Only the certificates of the POF holding the shares may be used, so that trading among certificates of different Funds will be stimulated. However, no more than ten certificates for purchasing shares in a particular company may be presented.[12] Each certificate may be used only once for the shares in that company and the total value of the discount can be no more than the "market value" of the certificates.

Outstanding issues

Whether the new Romanian institutions will be able to execute the complex tasks expected of them successfully is uncertain at the moment: many essential elements are not yet in place. In weighing the balance of risks it is useful to pose several inter-related questions about the new economic organisation and institutions: will the institutional design result in a centralised or decentralised approach? What will the strategy be toward restructuring, and which institutions will be responsible? Will the SOF and POFs impose market-oriented corporate governance through the design of managements contracts, maintaining financial discipline and encouraging competitive behaviour? And will the process of actual privatisation (*i.e.* establishing owners interested in increasing their wealth) be accelerated? Put another way, will these institutions contribute to establishing market relations or merely perpetuate governmental control and a culture of enterprise dependency?

One of the most attractive features of the Romanian mass privatisation programme is the potential for decentralisation. At the time of writing there was still some confusion remaining over the role of the Ministries and the Funds, especially the SOF, particularly in the area of restructuring. The implication of the privatisation legislation and subsequent regulation is that the SOF (and even the POFs, though to a limited extent) would have responsibility for restructuring and that

Ministries were to confine themselves to overall policy. But this interpretation is by no means firmly established. Some Ministries clearly regard themselves as responsible for formulating enterprise and sectoral strategy – all in the name of industrial policy – even at a rather detailed level, viewing the Funds as being in the way of an execution agency, albeit under the regulatory control of the NAP.

A significant risk at present is that the SOF will dominate the POFs. This is partly a result of its earlier establishment and greater technical capability at the current time. This may only be temporary, but the delay in establishing shareholders' agreements for devolving medium-sized firms to the POFs, and the almost exclusive dominance of the SOF in the question of privatising small firms is worrying. Risks of perverse outcomes are lower with the POFs since, with appropriate design, they could be encouraged to foster management initiative and therefore market processes. A more determined effort to establish the POFs appears to be necessary.

The current state of uncertainty over institutional responsibilities is most apparent in the area of restructuring. In its current form the SOF has neither the staff, capability, nor financial resources to implement restructuring. To rectify this it would be necessary to transfer substantial sections of the Ministry of Industry and the Ministry of Agriculture to the SOF, a time-consuming process which could delay privatisation. In this variant there is a risk that the SOF could simply become a new super ministry – unless its constitution and operating rules are carefully defined. Alternatively, restructuring could be retained by the government. This should entail a transfer of such firms to the Ministries, leaving the SOF with clear-cut privatisation responsibilities. In this arrangement, unless a clear division were to be made, the probability of firms lobbying ministries to delay privatisation pending restructuring would be great. A process led by the Ministries is liable to be captured by the strong interest group structure, long entrenched there, though capture is also a risk with the SOF. At the time of writing, the government was considering plans for a separate Restructuring Agency.[13]

Restructuring of enterprises by the Ministries or by the SOF are similar in that they both favour centralised solutions. Concomitantly, they view restructuring as essentially a technological process, not simply a matter of cleaning up balance sheets and reorganizing firms and sectors, but involving major new investments in strategic sectors of the economy, along the lines of an industrial policy drawn up by the government. This approach ignores the option of devolving restructuring onto the firms themselves. A firm-based approach would promote institutional pluralism and hasten the transition to market relations: it would require that the role of the Funds be supplemented by active participation of banks, which play little explicit role in the current scheme, in evaluating individual firm proposals. The organisation of the SOF, and its institutional capacities, would be quite different from that currently being contemplated.

Corporate governance will not be improved in the market-oriented sense unless the performance criteria to be used by both the POF and the SOF are appropriately defined. From a market-based perspective, the Funds should focus on rate of return to investment and financial discipline. However, there is very little reason for the Funds to adopt such criteria; there is no shareholder pressure while the political control of the SOF (the Board of Governors is appointed by Parliament, the government and the President and is recallable) could expose it to the danger of becoming an arm of politically-oriented industrial policy. A manifestation of such influence would be a resort to quantitative indicators and other *ad hoc* interventions.[14] Reinforcing the risk that the development of market- and efficiency-oriented management could be retarded is the assumption in much of the legislation that firms would mainly be reinvesting rather than paying dividends; this does not contribute to introducing the rate of return into enterprise decisions. A positive feature of the programme, on the other hand, is the proposal that compensation of Fund directors and staff should contain both fixed and variable parts, the latter potentially being linked to the number of firms privatised. Remuneration is apparently still open to discussion but will have to be quite carefully considered if the absence of external market pressure on the Funds is to be compensated through internal managerial incentives.[15]

With ownership being vested in the POFs and the SOF there is a possibility that the new bankruptcy law will in fact be inoperative, the Funds not being prepared to allow one of their own firms to initiate an action against another.[16] This would not necessarily be bad if the Funds were to fulfil the institutional role of receiver and liquidator and, most importantly, if firms regarded this as credible. The great risk is that they will not and will simply see themselves as operating divisions of a still larger enterprise and therefore not subject to financial discipline. Moreover, the plethora of government decrees and committees designed to solve financial blockage could only serve to further confuse lines of responsibility.

Competitive behaviour by Romanian firms needs to be fostered, but it is uncertain whether the Funds will contribute to this process if the shareholders' agreements are implemented as envisaged. Due to the specialisation of POFs by both branch and region, they will become either national or regional monopoly owners. The POFs may of course choose not to exercise this potential power and act instead as owners at "arm's length" but, from the perspective of institutional design, it is useful to question whether there are sufficiently strong incentives for doing so. If the POFs were to be concerned about their sales proceeds – their raison d'être is to maximize the wealth of their certificate holders – then there may be an incentive to minimise competition between firms under their ownership and to lobby against price liberalisation. The risk is heightened by widespread popular feelings that competition is in any case wasteful and, more importantly, by the lack of an effective competition law and competition authority.[17] In the case of the SOF, the risk of non-competitive behaviour is more compelling. The SOF will be in control of large firms which are already highly concentrated and indeed are often monopolists or monopsonists. Selective deconcentration will certainly be required from the competition and efficiency aspects but may nevertheless be opposed by the new institution intent on avoiding "wasteful competition" and in preserving perceived synergies. The risk of such a course of behaviour would increase if trade policy were to come under direct or indirect control of the SOF. Once again it is important to stress that these are only risks: the legislative requirement that privatisation be completed in seven years and the need for yearly privatisation programmes might ensure other behaviour but this is uncertain.

A potentially important influence on institutional behaviour will be the relation between banks and the Funds – both *de facto* and *de jure*. At the time of writing, only the ownership relation between banks and the POFs had been settled with the 30 per cent shareholding in each bank being divided equally between the five Funds. The question of the control over the remaining 70 per cent was left in abeyance and was not automatically transferred to the SOF. Should the SOF receive this ownership share, the potential for the development of an "in-house bank" controlled by the industrial enterprises exists. Experience with this in other countries has been universally poor and especially where the holding company itself is not subject to binding financial restrictions. The probability of such an event is high, since the SOF is being burdened with substantial "restructuring" responsibilities without clearly defined financing; the prospect of financing restructuring from privatisation proceeds alone is improbable as is the prospect that this could be used as the budget restriction to control SOF actions. The balance of risk is further affected by the present lack of NBR regulations on related lending. The risk which should be avoided above all is concentrating all decision-making and resources on one institution (*i.e.* the SOF). The development of banks as independent centres of expertise would minimise the possibility of overall institutional failure.

Many of the above issues would be less important if the real privatisation process were to move faster as a result of the Funds and the use of vouchers. Despite the legislative restriction of seven years for the SOF, there is a possibility that the process could be quite slow. This is because the certificate system does not dispense with the time-consuming and controversial issue of valuation. Additional cash payments are involved (indeed this is essential to the support of the Funds including the SOF) while the system is not based on exhaustive auctions. There will therefore be a great tendency to place a high value on the state patrimony. In addition, with the employee buyout of small firms, all the issues of insider information are still present. It remains to be seen whether the formulation of annual privatisation plans will be no more than that or whether these plans will also be associated with pressure to lower selling prices so as actually to achieve privatisation objectives.

Notes and references

1. In this respect they resemble the Treuhandanstalt in Germany rather than the privatisation agencies in most other CEECs. For a comparison of institutions see *Privatisation Trends,* OECD, Paris, 1993. In addition, the National Agency for Privatisation will act as a regulator between the SOF and POFs.

2. Assets were revalued in late 1992 using replacement values to compensate for inflation established by the Ministry of Finance. These were not permitted to affect depreciation calculations.

3. Reports indicate that some managers are holding up title transfer as leverage to gain management contracts.

4. Indeed in early 1993, following the inauguration of a new government in late 1992, the Parliament changed four of the seventeen members of the newly-established board for the SOF. A proposal has been submitted to make some changes in the boards of POFs.

5. The Certificate of Ownership gives each holder one share in each of the five POFs. In the text such shares will be referred to as "certificates" to avoid confusion between them and shares of enterprises held by the POFs or SOF.

6. The Funds have been founded in separate cities.

7. The Savings Bank has since been withdrawn from the programme so that it can be more directly utilised to support the budget. Many strategic or critical sections such as energy, mining, telecommunications, and refining are *régies autonomes* and are therefore excluded from the programme.

8. Enterprises classed as medium-sized comprise firms not requiring significant restructuring, not dependent on the activity of large companies and operating in sectors with more than three producers (*i.e.* the Romanian definition of "competitive"). Around 3 000 out of 3 229 enterprises listed in Table III.1 by some accounts. See *Privatisation Project Romania,* Report No. 3, Voucher and Mass Privatisation Programmes in Romania, May 1992.

9. One possible advantage of the scheme is that as only vouchers are involved, the fund could feel itself less constrained by concepts of an appropriate price and therefore decrease the share price until the shares were sold. It is not obvious that this will occur since the fund has an interest in receiving cash rather than vouchers for the shares.

10. Certificates can only be used to pay for the 30 per cent share owned by the POF. The 70 per cent ownership of the SOF must be acquired with cash or credit.

11. The voucher holders who are employees or management of the enterprise to be sold will receive an extra 10 per cent discount to purchase up to 10 per cent of the shares offered for sale.

12. Reasons for this restriction vary. According to the NAP it is to encourage widespread ownership. Other sources maintain that it was to prevent "speculation".

13. The relationship of this proposal to the plan to place loss-making firms under a restructuring agency, as part of the plan to impose financial discipline, is unclear.

14. For an illustration of the problems arising from politically controlled holding companies and the associated politicisation of industry see *Economic Survey of Italy,* OECD, 1991.

15. Although not yet operational, the most advanced incentive system for management would appear to be that developed for the Polish mass privatisation funds. See *Economic Survey of Poland,* OECD, 1992.

16. The Treuhandanstalt in Germany, which to some extent has been used as a prototype in developing the SOF, in fact instructed its enterprises not to initiate bankruptcy proceedings against each other. See *Economic Survey of Germany,* OECD, 1991.

17. The Treuhandanstalt is a sole owner with the potential to restrict competition between firms. However, it is subject to two powerful competition authorities (both German and of the European Community) which have challenged several of its actions. Reforms of Polish industry are also subject to an independent competition authority.

Publications in the CCEET Series

Bulgaria - An Economic Assessment (1992) Format 16X23
(14 92 05 1) ISBN 92-64-13753-X   FF90   £13.00   US$23.00   DM37

OECD Economic Surveys/CCEET. 1991-1992 Series:
Poland (1992) Format 16X23
(09 92 03 1) ISBN 92-64-13723-8   FF90   £13.00   US$20.00   DM37

Hungary (1991) Format 16X23
(09 92 01 1) ISBN 92-64-13554-5   FF90   £13.00   US$20.00   DM37

Czech and Slovak Federal Republic (1991) Format 16X23
(09 92 02 1) ISBN 92-64-13607-X   FF90   £13.00   US$20.00   DM37

Price for the three surveys: Hungary, Poland,
Czech and Slovak Federal Republic   FF230   £32.00   US$52.00   DM95

National Accounts for the Former Soviet Union
(1993) Format16X23
(14 93 03 1) ISBN 92-64-13856-0   FF150   £25.00   US$35.00   DM60

Short-Term Economic Statistics -- Central and Eastern Europe
(1992) (Bilingual) Format 16X23. Also available on Diskette
(14 92 01 3) ISBN 92-64-03523-0   FF 120   £ 16.00   US$ 32.00   DM 48

The Transition to a Market Economy:
Volume 1 -- The Broad Issues.
Volume 2 -- Special Issues (CCEET)
(1992)   (Bilingual) Format 16X23. Two volumes not sold separately
(14 91 06 3) ISBN 92-64-03520-6   FF300   £42.00   US$72.00   DM12

MAIN SALES OUTLETS OF OECD PUBLICATIONS
PRINCIPAUX POINTS DE VENTE DES PUBLICATIONS DE L'OCDE

ARGENTINA – ARGENTINE
Carlos Hirsch S.R.L.
Galería Güemes, Florida 165, 4° Piso
1333 Buenos Aires   Tel. (1) 331.1787 y 331.2391
                                    Telefax: (1) 331.1787

AUSTRALIA – AUSTRALIE
D.A. Information Services
648 Whitehorse Road, P.O.B 163
Mitcham, Victoria 3132   Tel. (03) 873.4411
                                    Telefax: (03) 873.5679

AUSTRIA – AUTRICHE
Gerold & Co.
Graben 31
Wien I   Tel. (0222) 533.50.14

BELGIUM – BELGIQUE
Jean De Lannoy
Avenue du Roi 202
B-1060 Bruxelles   Tel. (02) 538.51.69/538.08.41
                                Telefax: (02) 538.08.41

CANADA
Renouf Publishing Company Ltd.
1294 Algoma Road
Ottawa, ON K1B 3W8   Tel. (613) 741.4333
                                      Telefax: (613) 741.5439
Stores:
61 Sparks Street
Ottawa, ON K1P 5R1   Tel. (613) 238.8985
211 Yonge Street
Toronto, ON M5B 1M4   Tel. (416) 363.3171
                                      Telefax: (416)363.59.63

Les Éditions La Liberté Inc.
3020 Chemin Sainte-Foy
Sainte-Foy, PQ G1X 3V6   Tel. (418) 658.3763
                                      Telefax: (418) 658.3763

Federal Publications
165 University Avenue
Toronto, ON M5H 3B8   Tel. (416) 581.1552
                                      Telefax: (416) 581.1743

Les Publications Fédérales
1185 Avenue de l'Université
Montréal, PQ H3B 3A7   Tel. (514) 954.1633
                                    Telefax : (514) 954.1633

CHINA – CHINE
China National Publications Import
Export Corporation (CNPIEC)
16 Gongti E. Road, Chaoyang District
P.O. Box 88 or 50
Beijing 100704 PR   Tel. (01) 506.6688
                                      Telefax: (01) 506.3101

DENMARK – DANEMARK
Munksgaard Export and Subscription Service
35, Nørre Søgade, P.O. Box 2148
DK-1016 København K   Tel. (33) 12.85.70
                                      Telefax: (33) 12.93.87

FINLAND – FINLANDE
Akateeminen Kirjakauppa
Keskuskatu 1, P.O. Box 128
00100 Helsinki   Tel. (358 0) 12141
                                      Telefax: (358 0) 121.4441

FRANCE
OECD/OCDE
Mail Orders/Commandes par correspondance:
2, rue André-Pascal
75775 Paris Cedex 16   Tel. (33-1) 45.24.82.00
Telefax: (33-1) 45.24.81.76   or (33-1) 45.24.85.00
                                Telex: 640048 OCDE

OECD Bookshop/Librairie de l'OCDE :
33, rue Octave-Feuillet
75016 Paris   Tel. (33-1) 45.24.81.67
                                    (33-1) 45.24.81.81

Documentation Française
29, quai Voltaire
75007 Paris   Tel. 40.15.70.00
Gibert Jeune (Droit-Économie)
6, place Saint-Michel
75006 Paris   Tel. 43.25.91.19
Librairie du Commerce International
10, avenue d'Iéna
75016 Paris   Tel. 40.73.34.60
Librairie Dunod
Université Paris-Dauphine
Place du Maréchal de Lattre de Tassigny
75016 Paris   Tel. 47.27.18.56
Librairie Lavoisier
11, rue Lavoisier
75008 Paris   Tel. 42.65.39.95
Librairie L.G.D.J. - Montchrestien
20, rue Soufflot
75005 Paris   Tel. 46.33.89.85
Librairie des Sciences Politiques
30, rue Saint-Guillaume
75007 Paris   Tel. 45.48.36.02
P.U.F.
49, boulevard Saint-Michel
75005 Paris   Tel. 43.25.83.40
Librairie de l'Université
12a, rue Nazareth
13100 Aix-en-Provence   Tel. (16) 42.26.18.08
Documentation Française
165, rue Garibaldi
69003 Lyon   Tel. (16) 78.63.32.23
Librairie Decitre
29, place Bellecour
69002 Lyon   Tel. (16) 72.40.54.54

GERMANY – ALLEMAGNE
OECD Publications and Information Centre
August-Bebel-Allee 6
D-W 5300 Bonn 2   Tel. (0228) 959.120
                                      Telefax: (0228) 959.12.17

GREECE – GRÈCE
Librairie Kauffmann
Mavrokordatou 9
106 78 Athens   Tel. 322.21.60
                                      Telefax: 363.39.67

HONG-KONG
Swindon Book Co. Ltd.
13–15 Lock Road
Kowloon, Hong Kong   Tel. 366.80.31
                                      Telefax: 739.49.75

HUNGARY – HONGRIE
Euro Info Service
POB 1271
1464 Budapest   Tel. (1) 111.62.16
                                      Telefax : (1) 111.60.61

ICELAND – ISLANDE
Mál Mog Menning
Laugavegi 18, Pósthólf 392
121 Reykjavik   Tel. 162.35.23

INDIA – INDE
Oxford Book and Stationery Co.
Scindia House
New Delhi 110001   Tel.(11) 331.5896/5308
                                      Telefax: (11) 332.5993
17 Park Street
Calcutta 700016   Tel. 240832

INDONESIA – INDONÉSIE
Pdii-Lipi
P.O. Box 269/JKSMG/88
Jakarta 12790   Tel. 583467
                                      Telex: 62 875

IRELAND – IRLANDE
TDC Publishers – Library Suppliers
12 North Frederick Street
Dublin 1   Tel. 74.48.35/74.96.77
                                      Telefax: 74.84.16

ISRAEL
Electronic Publications only
Publications électroniques seulement
Sophist Systems Ltd.
71 Allenby Street
Tel-Aviv 65134   Tel. 3-29.00.21
                                      Telefax: 3-29.92.39

ITALY – ITALIE
Libreria Commissionaria Sansoni
Via Duca di Calabria 1/1
50125 Firenze   Tel. (055) 64.54.15
                                      Telefax: (055) 64.12.57
Via Bartolini 29
20155 Milano   Tel. (02) 36.50.83
Editrice e Libreria Herder
Piazza Montecitorio 120
00186 Roma   Tel. 679.46.28
                                      Telefax: 678.47.51
Libreria Hoepli
Via Hoepli 5
20121 Milano   Tel. (02) 86.54.46
                                      Telefax: (02) 805.28.86
Libreria Scientifica
Dott. Lucio de Biasio 'Aeiou'
Via Coronelli, 6
20146 Milano   Tel. (02) 48.95.45.52
                                      Telefax: (02) 48.95.45.48

JAPAN – JAPON
OECD Publications and Information Centre
Landic Akasaka Building
2-3-4 Akasaka, Minato-ku
Tokyo 107   Tel. (81.3) 3586.2016
                                      Telefax: (81.3) 3584.7929

KOREA – CORÉE
Kyobo Book Centre Co. Ltd.
P.O. Box 1658, Kwang Hwa Moon
Seoul   Tel. 730.78.91
                                      Telefax: 735.00.30

MALAYSIA – MALAISIE
Co-operative Bookshop Ltd.
University of Malaya
P.O. Box 1127, Jalan Pantai Baru
59700 Kuala Lumpur
Malaysia   Tel. 756.5000/756.5425
                                      Telefax: 757.3661

MEXICO – MEXIQUE
Revistas y Periodicos Internacionales S.A. de C.V.
Florencia 57 - 1004
Mexico, D.F. 06600   Tel. 207.81.00
                                      Telefax : 208.39.79

NETHERLANDS – PAYS-BAS
SDU Uitgeverij
Christoffel Plantijnstraat 2
Postbus 20014
2500 EA's-Gravenhage   Tel. (070 3) 78.99.11
Voor bestellingen: Tel. (070 3) 78.98.80
                                      Telefax: (070 3) 47.63.51

NEW ZEALAND
NOUVELLE-ZÉLANDE
Legislation Services
P.O. Box 12418
Thorndon, Wellington   Tel. (04) 496.5652
                                      Telefax: (04) 496.5698

NORWAY – NORVÈGE
Narvesen Info Center – NIC
Bertrand Narvesens vei 2
P.O. Box 6125 Etterstad
0602 Oslo 6   Tel. (02) 57.33.00
                              Telefax: (02) 68.19.01

PAKISTAN
Mirza Book Agency
65 Shahrah Quaid-E-Azam
Lahore 54000   Tel. (42) 353.601
                              Telefax: (42) 231.730

PHILIPPINE – PHILIPPINES
International Book Center
5th Floor, Filipinas Life Bldg.
Ayala Avenue
Metro Manila   Tel. 81.96.76
                              Telex 23312 RHP PH

PORTUGAL
Livraria Portugal
Rua do Carmo 70-74
Apart. 2681
1117 Lisboa Codex   Tel.: (01) 347.49.82/3/4/5
                              Telefax: (01) 347.02.64

SINGAPORE – SINGAPOUR
Information Publications Pte. Ltd.
41, Kallang Pudding, No. 04-03
Singapore 1334   Tel. 741.5166
                              Telefax: 742.9356

SPAIN – ESPAGNE
Mundi-Prensa Libros S.A.
Castelló 37, Apartado 1223
Madrid 28001   Tel. (91) 431.33.99
                              Telefax: (91) 575.39.98

Libreria Internacional AEDOS
Consejo de Ciento 391
08009 – Barcelona   Tel. (93) 488.34.92
                              Telefax: (93) 487.76.59

Llibreria de la Generalitat
Palau Moja
Rambla dels Estudis, 118
08002 – Barcelona
              (Subscripcions) Tel. (93) 318.80.12
              (Publicacions) Tel. (93) 302.67.23
                              Telefax: (93) 412.18.54

SRI LANKA
Centre for Policy Research
c/o Colombo Agencies Ltd.
No. 300-304, Galle Road
Colombo 3   Tel. (1) 574240, 573551-2
                     Telefax: (1) 575394, 510711

SWEDEN – SUÈDE
Fritzes Fackboksföretaget
Box 16356
Regeringsgatan 12
103 27 Stockholm   Tel. (08) 690.90.90
                              Telefax: (08) 20.50.21

Subscription Agency-Agence d'abonnements
Wennergren-Williams AB
P.O. Box 1305
171 25 Solna   Tel. (08) 705.97.50
                              Téléfax : (08) 27.00.71

SWITZERLAND – SUISSE
Maditec S.A. (Books and Periodicals - Livres
et périodiques)
Chemin des Palettes 4
Case postale 2066
1020 Renens 1   Tel. (021) 635.08.65
                              Telefax: (021) 635.07.80

Librairie Payot S.A.
4, place Pépinet
1003 Lausanne   Tel. (021) 341.33.48
                              Telefax: (021) 341.33.45

Librairie Unilivres
6, rue de Candolle
1205 Genève   Tel. (022) 320.26.23
                              Telefax: (022) 329.73.18

Subscription Agency - Agence d'abonnement
Dynapresse Marketing S.A.
38 avenue Vibert
1227 Carouge   Tel.: (022) 308.07.89
                              Telefax : (022) 308.07.99

See also – Voir aussi :
OECD Publications and Information Centre
August-Bebel-Allee 6
D-W 5300 Bonn 2 (Germany) Tel. (0228) 959.120
                              Telefax: (0228) 959.12.17

TAIWAN – FORMOSE
Good Faith Worldwide Int'l. Co. Ltd.
9th Floor, No. 118, Sec. 2
Chung Hsiao E. Road
Taipei   Tel. (02) 391.7396/391.7397
                              Telefax: (02) 394.9176

THAILAND – THAÏLANDE
Suksit Siam Co. Ltd.
113, 115 Fuang Nakhon Rd.
Opp. Wat Rajbopith
Bangkok 10200   Tel. (662) 251.1630
                              Telefax: (662) 236.7783

TURKEY – TURQUIE
Kültür Yayinlari Is-Türk Ltd. Sti.
Atatürk Bulvari No. 191/Kat 13
Kavaklidere/Ankara   Tel. 428.11.40 Ext. 2458
Dolmabahce Cad. No. 29
Besiktas/Istanbul   Tel. 260.71.88
                              Telex: 43482B

UNITED KINGDOM – ROYAUME-UNI
HMSO
Gen. enquiries   Tel. (071) 873 0011
Postal orders only:
P.O. Box 276, London SW8 5DT
Personal Callers HMSO Bookshop
49 High Holborn, London WC1V 6HB
                              Telefax: (071) 873 8200
Branches at: Belfast, Birmingham, Bristol, Edin-
burgh, Manchester

UNITED STATES – ÉTATS-UNIS
OECD Publications and Information Centre
2001 L Street N.W., Suite 700
Washington, D.C. 20036-4910 Tel. (202) 785.6323
                              Telefax: (202) 785.0350

VENEZUELA
Libreria del Este
Avda F. Miranda 52, Aptdo. 60337
Edificio Galipán
Caracas 106   Tel. 951.1705/951.2307/951.1297
                     Telegram: Libreste Caracas

Subscription to OECD periodicals may also be
placed through main subscription agencies.

Les abonnements aux publications périodiques de
l'OCDE peuvent être souscrits auprès des
principales agences d'abonnement.

Orders and inquiries from countries where Distribu-
tors have not yet been appointed should be sent to:
OECD Publications Service, 2 rue André-Pascal,
75775 Paris Cedex 16, France.

Les commandes provenant de pays où l'OCDE n'a
pas encore désigné de distributeur devraient être
adressées à : OCDE, Service des Publications,
2, rue André-Pascal, 75775 Paris Cedex 16, France.

04-1993

OECD PUBLICATIONS, 2 rue André-Pascal, 75775 PARIS CEDEX 16
PRINTED IN FRANCE
(14 93 08 1) ISBN 92-64-13939-7 - No. 46649 1993